MANAGING
THE MANAGERS

MANAGING
THE MANAGERS

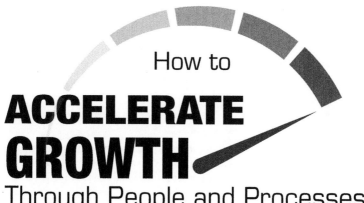

How to

ACCELERATE
GROWTH
Through People and Processes

with 35-57 Employees

LAURIE L. TAYLOR

Printed in the United States of America.

ISBN: 978-1973772064

This publication is designed to provide accurate and authoritative information in regard to the subject matter covered. It is sold with the understanding that the publisher is not engaged in rendering legal, accounting, or other professional services. If legal advice or other expert assistance is required, the services of a competent professional person should be sought.

TABLE OF CONTENTS

INTRODUCTION

In Stage 4, with 35 – 57 employees, you need managers who "have been there, done that."

This isn't the time to think about saving money by hiring inexperienced managers. Your leadership skills will be put to the test along with your ability to put your ego aside and hire people who know more than you do (and who expect a pretty good-sized paycheck in return!).

Still hanging onto your need to control everything? Still playing specialist or out there "visioning" your next opportunity? Sorry – wrong time, wrong focus.

By the 4th stage of growth, you are now spending at least 70% of your time "managing." Getting the right people on board to take the company through this stage is all about bringing on experienced managers, putting effective procedures in place, creating management systems and maintaining your market position.

Effective communication is critical. Three out of your five top challenges require a plan that keeps everyone up to speed on what's going on, and with 35 – 57 employees, that isn't easy.

As you moved through Stage 3, you learned how to "let it go to let it grow," and you did well! You learned to trust your people by setting clear expectations and managing to those expectations. You now have a company that doesn't rely on you 100% to make all the decisions.

Your big challenge in Stage 4 is learning how to "manage your managers" without abdicating authority and responsibility. As with many aspects of growing a business, it's harder than it sounds.

As you begin to hire people more skilled in different aspects of your business, there will be a tendency to want to let them do what you've hired them to do. If sales is not your passion, hiring that gunslinger sales manager can feel like you've found the pot of gold at the end of the proverbial rainbow. You haven't.

When the marketing communications company I helped grow from a startup hit Stage 4, we decided to hire a sales manager to oversee our small sales staff. My business partner was incredibly good at sales but we knew, in order to grow, we had to expand our sales force and find someone to manage that department.

> **If sales is not your passion, hiring that gunslinger sales manager can feel like you've found the pot of gold at the end of the proverbial rainbow. You haven't.**

When your CEO, the face of the company is also your top sales person, many issues crop up. One of the biggest challenges was managing the handoff from the CEO (also, the sales person) to one of our account managers. Clients who had started out with the CEO didn't want to deal with anyone else. The attachment hurdle created other issues and our CEO became the bottleneck in our project management system. She couldn't manage all the work she was creating, the client's work started to suffer, and deadlines became too fluid.

Our goal was to hire a sales manager who would drive sales and slowly remove our CEO from the process. We decided on an experienced sales manager from a large corporate environment. That, as it turned out, was our biggest mistake (among many others).

In our attempt to remove our CEO from direct sales activities, we made several assumptions. The first was that since our new sales manager was experienced in sales, we would focus on helping her learn our service offerings. We didn't train her on how our company solved customer problems.

The reality was, we micromanaged this person from the beginning. The subtle message we sent as she attempted to find her own way was "that's not how we do things here." Our CEO left little room for the new sales manager to gain confidence in her own right. The CEO went on sales calls and stepped all over the presentations, which caused resentment on both sides.

Ultimately, we didn't do our homework on this critical hire. We were looking for a quick solution but what we learned is there aren't any when you are growing a company. We wanted to remove our CEO from sales for the good of the company. We didn't realize how hard it would be.

As you think about hiring and training managers in this stage of growth, think through the ramifications it can have on the organization.

- Are critical processes written down so someone new can come in and understand what they need to do to succeed?
  - We never captured our sales process. Our CEO "just made it happen."

- Is the person currently responsible for the job duties prepared to train and mentor a new hire?
  - We didn't factor time into the CEO's schedule to train and mentor. The expectation was the new person could learn by watching and listening.

- Can you maintain revenues and expenses as a critical position is transitioned to a new person?
  - We panicked. When the new sales person wasn't as good as our CEO in closing business, our sales took a dive and we reacted by letting the sales manager go.

We learned some very hard lessons as we transitioned from Stage 3 to Stage 4. Eventually, we hired another sales manager, fixed our project management process, created a training program for all new and existing employees and budgeted for talent we knew we needed.

As companies grow, the complexity level of the organization increases. That complexity level doesn't increase because of revenues, profits, or equity growth. Complexity increases because of the one factor in a company that is the hardest to control: people!

Study after study proves that the way to generate sustainable profits is to build the kind of work environment that attracts, focuses, and retains talented employees.

James Fischer, author of the book, *Navigating the Growth Curve*, discovered that as companies add more people to the equation, the dynamics change. Fischer developed the 7 Stages of Growth to address entrepreneurial companies struggling to

> Complexity increases because of the one factor in a company that is the hardest to control: people!

manage growth, from 1 – 500 employees. I worked with him for five years as a managing partner at Origin Institute.

Through my current company, FlashPoint!, I have spoken to thousands of CEOs regarding the unique 7 Stages of Growth business model. The information resonates with CEOs immediately.

At a presentation to over a hundred CEOs, a seasoned CEO, now running his twelfth company, said:

> *"After eighteen years of doing turnarounds and twelve years of investment banking, I finally found a system that prescribes the ideal management styles and focus for different sized companies. I am on the board of a private company and will be applying the Stages of Growth techniques when advising this company."*

This reaction is typical from a CEO who has been around the block, who understands the challenges of growing a successful company and who understands that simply reading the next how-to, book of the month isn't a formula for building a successful company.

The 7 Stages of Growth gets CEO's attention because the concepts allow a business owner to do three things.

1. Predict how growth will impact them.
2. Get them focused on the right things at the right time.
3. Adapt to necessary changes as the company grows.

This model allows you to look at the past, the present and the future in order to better understand what hidden agents are impacting your ability to grow. Once you identify those hidden agents, and put a name to the underlying issues, you can solve them and move on.

The 7 Stages of Growth provides every single employee the ability to understand the challenges a company faces as it grows. Each challenge can be discussed in terms everyone understands, thereby taking the mystery out of running a company.

The impact of creating a "language of growth" starts with understanding that language doesn't *describe* a person's experience, it *defines* their experience. Change the language and you change the experience.

> *"Learning about the Entrepreneurial Stages of Growth in the Executive Forum has been a seminal event. Several members could identify what's been holding them back and what they need to change to move to the next level. For some, it's their CEO Modality, for others, it's a focus on their Key Challenges, and for others, it's more about the Builder/Protector ratio. For all members, the ability to see their company within the context of an overall process that all companies experience has been very enlightening and has encouraged them to communicate their priorities more boldly with their people."*
>
> -Lee H. Self, Renaissance EXECUTIVE FORUMS
> of Northern Virginia

I know business owners struggle to focus on the constant barrage of issues that come their way every day. A fast-growing enterprise can quickly grow beyond an owner's ability to manage everything.

This book addresses critical areas of focus for a Stage 4 Company. You may not define growth by the addition of employees. You may think growth means creating a business with a solid income for as long as you want it. Or, you may just be starting to consider the amazing possibilities your company has to offer and are looking for ways to manage it as you grow.

Because Fischer's model is built on the premise that additional people adds complexity, it must be a high priority to build the kind of environment that attracts, fosters, and retains talented employees. To that end, building a profitable company depends on your ability to manage people.

One of the rules that govern the 7 Stages of Growth is: What you don't get done in any stage of growth doesn't go away. As a Stage 4 Company, you may find value in reading my third book, *The Art of Delegation: How to Effectively Let Go to Grow with 20 – 34 Employees*. This book addresses issues you may have missed or ignored in an earlier stage of business growth.

> ## Building a profitable company depends on your ability to manage people.

In Stage 3, with 20 – 34 employees, it was all about delegation, all about you, the CEO letting go. The necessity of that lesson will become painfully clear if you head into Stage 4 looking like a cat dangling from your living room drapes – you have to LET GO!

Stage 4 owners must be prepared to manage employees that may know more than they do. As a Stage 4 owner, you may find yourself shelling out salaries that keep you awake at night but you're paying for skills you need to grow your organization. Successful CEOs surround themselves with knowledgeable, experienced people – they want to be challenged on decisions, knowing that the more diversity of ideas and even attitude they bring on board, the more depth they create in their organization.

Processes and systems must be in place to control quality so that projects/programs/services can be replicated. Processes and systems give your employees an opportunity to succeed at what you hired them to do, which means you can focus on the longer, more strategic view of where your company will be in 18 – 24 months.

This professional Stage of Growth comes with certain challenges that you, as a business owner, may not be prepared to deal with. In this book, I'll explain how you can utilize effective tools to help you create effective processes, stay in constant communication with your team, learn how to embrace managing people and not lose sight of the culture and the vision you worked so hard to create.

The result is yours to determine. You have taken the first step to developing a strong foundation by considering the research-proven concepts that support the 7 Stages of Growth enterprise development model. As your company continues to add employees, I hope you return to my websites often to learn more about the challenges of each of the 7 Stages of Growth.

I wish you success in growing your business!

Your Success. My Passion.

Laurie Taylor, President

FlashPoint! LLC

www.igniteyourbiz.com

www.growthcurvespecialists.com

www.destination-greatness.com

Chapter 1:
What a Stage 4
Company Looks Like

S tage 4 is all about internal focus, internal processes and finding professional managers who know how to get work done through people and processes.

Why is one of your challenges in Stage 4 "employee turnover"? Because if you don't have strong, experienced managers in place, your employees will leave. Remember, people stay at a company because they respect their manager. If you can provide your employees with managers who know how to manage the work of the company, as well as manage the people, your employees will feel less frustrated, work with clearly outlined expectations, work fewer hours, will be more productive and receive valuable input on their performance on a regular basis.

Stage 4 is also about helping managers feel confident about their team, about their work, and about their own identity as a team leader. Your job is to help them gain that confidence.

Don't worry about integrating these managers across the company just yet. Help them find their own way; work with them to be accountable as their team evolves and matures. You will avoid a lot of finger pointing and department disputes if you let each manager build a stronghold and develop their own sense of commitment and team-ness.

Are you getting the message? Managing the managers isn't just about training qualified people to move up in your organization.

As the Chief Operating Officer of a growing business, I often promoted top performers into management positions and often-times, it backfired. Worse, I took a highly functioning individual, who was very good at their job, and put them into a situation they were unprepared for. The impact those promotions had on our company was huge!

Managing is a tough job and we simply assumed the individual would "just get it." (People are not automatically good managers just because they are good at their job.) The employees suffered because the new manager was totally unprepared to suddenly give direction to people who had been their peers. Sometimes the person we promoted simply left out of frustration and we lost a great employee.

I understand the lure of a promotion. And I understand an organization's desire to want to promote from within. Good performance should be rewarded. Naturally, the opportunity to make more money and move up in the organization seems like a good offer. Who would turn that down?

Turning a great employee into a great manager can end badly if you don't ask a few critical questions upfront. To effectively promote a great performer into a management position you need a plan.

1. Does the person WANT to be a manager of people? Is it a goal they strive toward?
2. Does the person UNDERSTAND the role a manager plays in the development of people and processes?
3. Does the person have the DESIRE to help people succeed?
4. Does the person know how to BUILD systems to gain efficiency of scale?

Yes, promoting from within can be done. However, experience tells us that it's usually an easy way for a CEO to avoid doing the harder work of finding experienced, trained people who are hardwired to help them grow their business.

When you moved from Stage 3 to Stage 4, you went through what's called a Flood Zone, which is an increase in the level of activity. Because you are about to shift the major control of your company over to experienced managers, take time to review how the move will impact your company.

Ask yourself:

- Am I willing to hire people who have the skills and experience that I don't?
- Have I considered the impact on overhead and the ability to maintain profitability as I pay for experienced talent?
- Am I hiring the right people? How will I know?
- How confident am I as an effective and skilled manager?
- What is the plan to train new managers?

- Am I prepared to let go of processes that are no longer effective and put new ones in place?
- Am I watching the key indicators of success every day?
- Am I setting clear expectations and managing to those expectations?
- Do I understand my new role as I slowly release more responsibility to others?

In Stage 4, the company is much more complex. With up to 57 employees, there is no way the CEO can have her fingers in everything.

As the CEO of a Stage 4 company, 10% of your time should be devoted to fine-tuning the vision of the company, 20% should be spent as the technician or the specialist and 70% should be spent managing people. This percentage blend is referred to as the Three Faces of a Leader. Now is the time to examine your own leadership strengths and weaknesses.

In my book, *The Art of Delegation: How to Effectively Let Go to Grow with 20 – 34 Employees*, I spent time exploring the challenge all leaders face: how to delegate effectively. This challenge forces leaders to examine if they have the right people in the right seats. The act of delegation requires trust and if that trust isn't there, you'll never feel completely comfortable letting go. The reality is, you have to learn how to delegate to grow. Having the right people and processes in place is an important step toward letting go of control.

In his book, *Traction*, Gino Wickman talks about a leader's need to "rise to their Unique Ability®" as the company grows. Wickman verifies that by not delegating to the right people, you are holding your company back and perhaps setting yourself up for burnout. My business partner's Unique Ability was sales. We needed to find a sales manager to manage our sales team and free her up to concentrate on her other skills. We needed someone who could develop market expansion opportunities and maintain strong relationships with clients.

As hard as it is for founders to step aside from the work that has taken their company where it is, the rewards of releasing tasks and responsibilities to others who have different ideas and experience are immediate.

REQUIRED LEADERSHIP SKILLS

According to author and psychologist, Daniel Goleman, self-directed learning is a very effective management development tool. It is the act of intentionally developing or strengthening an aspect of who you are or who you want to be. By creating an environment that encourages learning, invites new and different ideas, and promotes an individual's desire to constantly improve, a Stage 4 leader can start to reap the rewards of a growing organization.

The required skills for a leader in Stage 4 are:

- The awareness to recognize a need for managerial sophistication
- The ability to release control to ever more competent managers
- The willingness to commit to new management systems and to intentionally manage growth
- The ability to see and correct personal management deficiencies

- The ability to set clear expectations and manage to those expectations

I promise, if you take the time to study the 5 Challenges outlined here and apply the strategies to overcome them, you will continue to build a foundation for your company; whether you stay in Stage 4 or grow your business up to Stage 7, with 161 – 500 employees.

> *"Nowhere have I ever found an incisive, insightful analytical tool like that offered by the 7 Stages of Growth. It makes charting a company's growth as easy as painting by numbers."*
>
> -David Zucker, *Chief Executive Officer,*
> Zocalo Community Development, Stage 3 Company

I know, because I've been there. As the owner and partner of a multi-million dollar company that I helped grow from two to over 100 employees, we struggled in Stage 4 for all of the reasons I cover in this book. In March of 2000, the false economy driven by the dot. com explosion collapsed. We had to lay off 30% of our staff and we struggled to stay afloat. Because we struggled, we lost critical traction. When you lose traction, you create chaos. If I had known then what I know now, I firmly believe we would not have had to negatively impact 30 people's lives.

PREDICTING GROWTH

Through presenting the 7 Stages of Growth to CEOs around the country, I've encountered two consistent character traits.

1. People who start or run a company are smart, energetic, capable, able to think outside the box, willing to put in long hours, have a strong vision, believe 150% in their product or service, and feel overwhelmed most of the time.

2. They want a structure they can utilize to predict what is coming, how to manage the hundreds of issues that pop up every day and how to make sure they survive to the next stage of the business growth cycle.

During the journey through the 5 Challenges presented in Stage 4, I guarantee to help you:

1. Focus on the immediate issues in front of you.
2. Predict how growth will impact you.
3. Adapt to the changes your company is going through.

In the early stages of growing a company, you need to ask core questions such as:

1. How do I plan on targeting, capturing and caring for my customers?
2. Where do I find qualified people?

3. How do I keep exceptional people?

4. Am I tracking my revenue by revenue groups in order to understand where I generate the best margins?

5. Are we horizontally or vertically integrated?

6. What is our dominant culture?

7. What are our core processes?

8. Where do we see our company in three to five years?

9. How will we capture and encourage knowledge?

10. What is the relationship our company has with the customer, our vendors, our allies, and our competitors?

This book is designed to help a Stage 4 CEO understand where to focus her energies to get the most traction as she moves from Delegation to the Professional stage of growth.

In Stage 4, the top gate of focus is Process. Therefore, all processes must be verified, efficient, up-to-date and contribute to the company's bottom line. However, process development and training will only keep a company sustainable and allow scalability when the right people are hired, engaged and developed.

In Stage 3, the top gate of focus was People, which should have been a wake-up call to recruit, hire, train and develop people for the positions that will take the company forward.

Because three of the top challenges for Stage 3 (with 20 – 34 employees) are Staff Buy-In, Leadership/Staff Communication Gap, and Unclear Values Throughout the Organization – all centered around people issues – you may want to read my book, *The Art of Delegation: How to Effectively Let Go to Grow with 20 – 34 Employees.* In it, I address how to overcome those challenges. Remember, what you don't get done in any one stage of growth, doesn't go away. If you haven't addressed critical people issues, make sure it is part of your tactical planning approach now.

When James Fischer interviewed growth-smart companies in his 7 Stages of Growth research study, he could identify 27 specific challenges that business owners experienced as they grew. Business owners find value in these 27 challenges because they finally have a starting point to talk about what's going on in their business.

Fischer referred to these as the "stages of growth challenges." His premise was that CEOs should focus on these critical challenges at each stage of growth to minimize the chaos that can create obstacles to growth.

Recently, one of my Growth Curve Specialists (GCS) conducted a Stages of Growth X-Ray™ with a non-profit group in Taipei, Taiwan. Since the research for the 7 Stages of Growth was all done in the United States, this was an opportunity to see how the concepts resonated in other cultures. The purpose of the X-Ray process is to create dialogue around critical issues and provide the entire team with a chance to share their own perspectives.

Steve Contival is the Executive Director of the YWAM (Youth With a Mission) in Taiwan. With the help of Ron Brewster, a Growth Curve Specialist, and Executive Director of the YWAM in San Diego, Steve's team assessed their own progress through five online surveys. Each survey provided participants with a chance to put a name to a

problem or concern and then to talk about the issues in a constructive two-day workshop.

It was interesting to know that businesses everywhere seem to
resonate with the challenges identified in the 7 Stages of Growth.
It's also encouraging to see how they evaluated their own progress as
they uncovered different obstacles and talked about the impact on
the organization.

> *"The Stages of Growth training came at a great time for us - both
> validating and putting vocabulary to things that we were all feeling
> and letting us see we were 'normal' - but also helping us recognize
> some things that were there but we weren't aware of. I'm very grateful
> we had this time and believe it would be helpful for people in any
> stage of growth."*
>
> — Scott Contival, *Executive Director,*
> YWAM, Taipei, Taiwan

It's hard for business owners, bombarded by issues every day,
to articulate what is going on for them. They know something is
creating a problem, but they can't identify what it is. The 27 Challenges define in a few words what business owners are experiencing.
That's a big step when you are trying to engage a team of people to
help you fix something. The value of understanding the stages of
growth is that throughout the model, we are guiding the CEO on
how to prioritize their time, energy and dollars.

In a Stage 4 company, the CEO needs to manage the managers
she has hired to provide direction. This is not the time to abdicate
authority or responsibility. It's even more important that the CEO

understands the value of setting clear expectations and managing to those expectations.

Throughout the research study, Fisher recognized that successful Stage 4 CEOs had figured out the importance of spending time and resources on getting the right procedures and systems in place. With 35 – 57 employees, you must get organized and ensure that work processes can be replicated efficiently to maintain a solid net profit. One of the top challenges focuses on project management and resource allocation issues.

As your company grows, you will eventually have to tackle all 27 Challenges.

THE 27 CHALLENGES

1. Profits are inadequate to grow the company
2. Need for an improved profit design
3. Customers are migrating away from your products/ services
4. Continual cash flow challenges
5. Limited capital available to grow
6. Employee turnover
7. Hiring quality staff
8. Staff morale and voltage challenges
9. Need for a flexible planning model
10. Need to have better staff buy-in
11. Project management & resource coordination challenges
12. Leadership/staff communication gap

13. New staff orientation

14. Staff training

15. Unclear values throughout the organization

16. Dealing with the cost of lost expertise or knowledge when employees leave

17. Chaotic periods destabilize company

18. Organization needs to understand how the company will grow in the future, not just the leadership

19. Organization needs to better understand the impact that staff satisfaction has on the company's profitability

20. Company culture is generally resistant to change

21. The marketplace and your customers change too quickly

22. Difficulty forecasting problem areas before they surface

23. Difficulty diagnosing the real problems or obstacles to growth

24. Too slow getting new products/services to market

25. Not able to quickly get systems and procedures in place as the company is growing

26. Weak product/service development and differentiation in market

27. Challenge expanding sales

THE TOP 5 CHALLENGES OF A STAGE 4 COMPANY

The ability to help a CEO get clear about the right things at the right time is what separates high performing companies from mediocre companies. The small percentage of companies that succeed are the ones that stay ahead of their growth curve.

The value of utilizing the 27 Challenges to navigate your own growth curve is clear. They:

- Force a company to put words to their critical top 5 issues
- Provide an opportunity to see how the leadership team defines the company's top challenges
- Force a discussion that moves the company toward alignment of goals and objectives
- Allow the leadership team to build confidence as they proactively tackle critical issues
- Force a deeper discussion about how to address each of the top 5 challenges
- Help the leadership team to address more strategic issues once everyone agrees to problems

The Top 5 Challenges for a Stage 4 Company, in this order, are:

1. Project management and resource allocation challenges
2. Difficulty diagnosing the real problems or obstacles to growth
3. Employee turnover
4. Not able to quickly get systems and procedures in place as the company grows
5. Organization needs to understand how the company will grow in the future

Chapter 2:
Key Growth Concepts

As a company navigates through Stage 4, its primary goal is to hire and/or train managers to run different aspects of the company. A CEO should evaluate how the company will grow and think about the following foundational building blocks.

FUNCTION	BUILDING BLOCKS
Management Systems	You should have a Performance Management System that addresses objectives, goals, measurement, feedback, evaluation and rewards. You should also have Project Management System templates.
Financial System	Your financial system should include a Profit Plan, Financial Modeling, a Cash Flow Forecast and Dashboard with Key Indicators for each division.
Team/Staff	Your hiring system should help you identify the skills and talent that are needed and then help you find, recruit, select and hire great employees. You should have a plan for each employee describing expectations, performance measurements and actions that will be taken to help him/her succeed.
Marketing/Sales	You should have a well-defined sales and marketing system that your sales people are using. It's time for a major upgrade of sales systems and probably your CRM system. You should have a Customer Intelligence System to stay abreast of your customers and market.
Decision Making Template	You should create, maintain and adhere to a strict decision-making template and evaluate decisions, good or bad, to ensure you know how to improve upon on-going decisions.

There are three additional concepts central to the Stages of Growth language: the 4 Rules that govern the 7 Stages of Growth, understanding the Transition Zones between stages and the Three Gates of Focus. These concepts were discussed in my other books that cover issues for Stages 1, 2 and 3 as well.

THE FOUR RULES THAT GOVERN THE 7 STAGES OF GROWTH

As a business owner navigates their own growth curve, there are four rules that help to walk that fine line between chaos and equilibrium.

RULE #1:

THE MOVEMENT FROM ONE STAGE OF GROWTH TO ANOTHER BEGINS AS SOON AS YOU LAND IN ANY STAGE OF GROWTH.

You don't become a Stage 4 company overnight. As soon as you enter Stage 3, you begin to be a Stage 4 company. Think of the Stages of Growth as a continuum. You are moving along this continuum based on your strategic plan.

If you are a Stage 3 company today, and plan to have 38 employees on board in 18 months, NOW is the time to plan. This is what sets the 7 Stages of Growth apart from other business models. A CEO can actually *predict* when they will move into another stage of growth and adjust to upcoming needs *before* they arrive.

RULE #2:

WHAT YOU DON'T GET DONE IN A SPECIFIC STAGE OF GROWTH DOES NOT GO AWAY.

The challenges for your current stage of growth need to be addressed before you move into a new stage of growth. For example, if you established your core values in Stage 3, one of the challenges identified for that stage of growth, you don't need to worry about them in Stage 4. If, however, you still are struggling with a Leadership/Staff Communication Gap, a challenge from Stage 3, you need to put additional focus on resolving that challenge today.

Business owners should consistently evaluate how well they are doing, not only with their current challenges, but also with the challenges that presented themselves in previous stages of growth.

Too often, we resolve surface issues without uncovering the root cause.

Focus on your specific People, Process and Profit/Revenue challenges so that you are well prepared for tomorrow. Remember, the complexity of an organization will always extract its due. Don't be lulled into a false sense of security; there is always a price to pay for rapid growth.

RULE #3:

TIME WILL MAKE A DIFFERENCE.

Each stage of growth has its own set of challenges. If you are a Stage 4 company with 38 employees and you've been that way for 15 years, time has allowed you to grow slowly and address challenges as you grew. However, if you grew quickly, blew through Stages 1, 2 and 3 and landed in Stage 4 overnight, there is a strong chance that the issues you should have addressed in Stage 3 remain unresolved.

The time rule applies to either slow or fast growth. It simply reminds you to pay attention to what you need to do as you grow through each stage of growth. A company that has been in one stage of growth for five years or more should look *ahead* to manage growth in a proactive way. Time makes a difference because slower growth is easier to manage.

Many companies choose to stay at a certain size. They prefer to grow in other dimensions, not in employees. Don't assume you have addressed your critical issues just because your business model limits the number of employees. Small companies are not immune to challenges simply because of low staff numbers.

RULE #4:
IF YOU AREN'T GROWING, YOU ARE DYING.

To stay fresh and current, something in your organization has to grow and change. The concept behind the stages of growth is similar to growth in nature, which has its own mechanisms to stir up the pot. A static condition in nature or in business is indicative of imminent death.

We are all familiar with the process a caterpillar goes through to turn into a butterfly. This is often described as one of the most intriguing transformations in the animal kingdom. If something goes wrong during the chrysalis stage, the butterfly will never emerge from the cocoon. Similarly, if the wheels start to come off a business in the early stages of growth, it may never recover.

As human beings, we have a tendency to gravitate toward a state of equilibrium because it is safe and understandable. In reality, if we stay in that state too long, it results in a slow dying away, just as it does in nature. Being able to get ahead of your growth curve allows you to recognize the signs of change and gives you time to react.

So, the answer to the question, "Do We Need to Grow?" is categorically YES. Even in a downturn economy when revenues are shrinking and profits melting away, there are areas of improvement a company can focus on.

The challenge for business owners in any stage of growth is to make sure they define growth for the company and not let growth define them.

CRITICAL TRANSITION ZONES

"Transition zones" exist between each stage of growth, which are actually phases of chaos an organization moves through in order to prepare itself for the next stage of growth. These transition zones are an important juncture in the growth model of any growing organization.

THE FLOOD ZONE

The transition zone between Stage 3 and Stage 4 is called the Flood Zone, named as such because the level of activity increases to the point where people can feel like they are drowning. There are more employees, more clients and more processes that need to be followed. The CEO's tendency is to add more people, but that only intensifies the problems.

This flood of activity will impact your small and growing team the hardest, especially if you haven't taken the time to upgrade your technology or improve your processes. A smooth transition requires an intentional plan to stay in touch with your employees and to effectively manage processes, sales and cash.

> The level of activity increases to the point where people can feel like they are drowning.

As a company moves from Stage 2 to Stage 3, it moves through a transition zone called a Wind Tunnel. It requires the leader to let go of methodologies that no longer work and acquire new ones that do.

A Flood Zone forces leadership to find new ways of dealing with the increased workload. Examine your processes and training programs, explore systems that track customer information and think about what positions you will need to hire when the time is right.

Here's an example of a Flood Zone in action. Let's look at a small service company in Colorado that's been in business for 20 years. A growth spurt took them from Stage 3 to Stage 4. It's a stable, well-run company with a strong and capable president and loyal employees.

An increase in customer accounts caused invoices and calls to suppliers to grow by 30%.

The CEO's wakeup call came when they were suddenly two weeks behind on invoicing. She knew revenues were growing but underestimated the impact the new growth would have on standard activities (such as invoicing). She couldn't control the Flood Zone, but she and her employees could have been better prepared if they had been able to identify the subtle changes that growth created.

During a Flood Zone, there is an increased level of confusion. Change occurs daily and employees start looking for someone to blame, usually through mumbled curses directed at leadership for putting them in this mess.

A good offense is better than a solid defense. Don't assume your staff is okay. Just because you understand the reality of growing a business, doesn't mean your employees do. Be aware that your employees are the ones who experience the increase in activity right away. They don't always know their limitations and are likely afraid to admit when they have issues.

This transition zone helps to create a language of growth, which allows employees to put a name to their pain and derive a measure of comfort. Utilize the language of growth to prepare employees for the chaos that

> Just because you understand the reality of growing a business, doesn't mean your employees do.

comes with change. Chaos is inevitable as a company grows. Take the time to explain to your staff what's going on when the company transitions through a Flood Zone on its way to Stage 4.

THE THREE GATES OF FOCUS: PROFIT/REVENUE, PEOPLE AND PROCESS

CEOs can use the Three Gates of Focus (Profit/Revenue, People and Process) to clarify the root cause of issues. When a CEO identifies the root cause, and helps employees do the same, issues are resolved sooner. Every issue you face in your organization can be categorized under one of the Three Gates. They are always stacked in the order of importance for a particular stage of growth. In Stage 4, the top gate of focus is Process.

◇◇

The **Process Gate** helps transform complexity into clarity through processes.
- Sales processes
- Marketing processes
- Financial processes
- Customer service processes
- Operational processes
- Management processes
- Risk management processes

The **People Gate** focuses on building competency, staff satisfaction, performance and innovation through the conscious development of people.
- Hiring and training
- Competitive benefits
- Ongoing, consistent training
- Employee engagement
- Vision, mission and core values
- Management training
- Leadership development
- Performance indicators
- Empowerment support

The **Profit/Revenue Gate** predicts growth by maximizing and anticipating profit/revenue and identifying capacity issues.

- Sales capacity
- Marketing capacity
- Facilities capacity
- Fulfillment capacity
- Capital availability
- Production capacity
- Product development capacity

Let's look at an example. Stan, a Stage 4 CEO, was aware that his employee, Rachel, was struggling with a project. Many CEOs blame the individual when there is a problem, instead of digging deeper to see if there is a process or a profit (can we afford it) issue.

To better understand Rachel's struggle, Stan asked, "Do you think your issue is People, Profit or Process related?

This specific question forced Rachel to think more seriously about the underlying issue and not just focus on what was showing up on the surface. Given the language, she may say that it's a People Issue and she needs more training; or she may identify that it's a Process Issue because the system she is using is no longer effective; or she may identify it as a Profit Issue, and explain that a critical piece of equipment is broken and needs to be replaced.

This brief but impactful conversation helped Stan adopt a problem-solving approach and gave Rachel a new way to approach the problem.

Language is the world's greatest change agent. Successful business owners instinctively know that you seed change in an enterprise by shifting and transforming the baseline language of the workplace community. People converse and communicate within the boundaries of the current language that describes their experience. Language doesn't just describe their experience; it *defines it*. Change the language and you change the experience.

For whatever reason, the financials of many businesses remain clouded in a language that confuses, rather than clarifies. Most people would prefer to leave this aspect up to the numbers people and be in the dark. Trying to explain a balance sheet to your employees is a little like trying to explain how an internal combustion engine works to someone who is not at all mechanically inclined. If, however, you explain there are drive mechanisms (spark plugs, gasoline, pistons, camshaft, transmission) that start the car moving forward, it all starts to make sense.

> Language doesn't just describe their experience; it *defines it*.

Adopt a similar approach when explaining to your employees that there are three ways to increase how much money you make: volume, price, and cost. You can increase the volume of what you sell; you can increase the sale price or decrease the production cost. Once your employees understand how they can directly impact these three factors, lights go on!

Suddenly, the financials are something they not only understand, but something they can talk about. The language shifts from the dry "earnings ratio to net profit" to a more engaged and educated interpretation. "We increased our price by 15%, increased our volume by 5%, decreased our costs by 20% and brought in an additional $50,000 in our first quarter." This is a powerful way to engage the entire company in understanding the financial impacts in your company.

One of the core values of the 7 Stages of Growth model is in its ability to help a company focus on the right things at the right time. The Gates of Focus allow everyone the opportunity to clarify issues quickly and reduce the chaos that comes with misdiagnosing a problem. In addition to providing clarity, the Three Gates of Focus begins the process of creating a language of growth. Throughout the 7 Stages, there are many opportunities for a CEO to help every employee understand what is going on in the company's growth cycle.

THREE GATES OF FOCUS FOR STAGE 1, STAGE 2, STAGE 3 AND STAGE 4

STAGE 1 1-10 EMPLOYEES	STAGE 2 11 – 19 EMPLOYEES	STAGE 3 20 – 34 EMPLOYEES	STAGE 4 35 – 57 EMPLOYEES
PROFIT/ REVENUE GATE	PROFIT/ REVENUE GATE	PEOPLE GATE	PROCESS GATE
PEOPLE GATE	PROCESS GATE	PROFIT/ REVENUE GATE	PROFIT/ REVENUE GATE
PROCESS GATE	PEOPLE GATE	PROCESS GATE	PEOPLE GATE

In Stage 4, the CEO needs to hire and train capable managers who she can trust to manage different aspects of the company. Because of the increase in the number of people, and the reality that processes are critical to ensure profitability and accountability, leadership has a lot to think about.

Simply hiring good managers isn't the end of story. The reality is that 70% of a CEOs time must be spent managing those managers. New managers need direction to move the company forward as they work with the CEO to strengthen processes, identify opportunities, and emulate the organization's culture and values.

Chapter 3:
Hidden Agents

What is a Hidden Agent? Hidden agents provide CEOs with a language to identify critical issues that may be creating obstacles to their growth. By understanding a company's hidden agents, a CEO can get to the root cause of a problem faster and engage their management team to focus on the right issues.

HIDDEN AGENT #1: BUILDER/ PROTECTOR RATIO

What do battlefield generals, sports coaches and successful business leaders have in common? They all methodically measure key indicators that reveal the health of the human psyche inside their organizations. These indicators predict the organization's ability to win (or not win) on any given day.

Good leaders measure the ratio between their company's *confidence* and *caution* as it directly reflects the outcome of their performance efforts. Otherwise known as the Builder/Protector ratio, it provides insight into the true balance of confidence (Builder) and caution (Protector) inside a company. This measurement allows a CEO and his/her leadership team to assess the company's ability to accept change and successfully navigate the change.

If you own a business, you more than likely already understand a Builder mentality. You create new ideas, take on new initiatives and find ways to expand revenue and profitability. You choose to challenge and improve the way things are done, thrive on risk and support growth initiatives.

A Protector mindset is cautious and prefers to slow down the pace of change. They are risk averse and highly suspicious of growth. Protectors generally don't feel confident in the company's financial strength and are slow to embrace optimism for the future.

The optimal Builder/Protector Ratio during Stage 4 is 3:2. The ratio changes according to the stage of growth you're in, and no other stage has this high of a Protector Ratio. Understanding why is important for a business owner to understand.

BUILDERS:

- Create new ideas
- Takes on new initiatives
- Find ways to expand revenue and profits
- Challenge the way things are done
- Are risk tolerant and highly supportive of growth
- Are highly confident
- Are always looking for new opportunities
- Don't back down from everyday challenges

PROTECTORS:

- Are cautious and slow paced
- Are risk averse
- May not feel confident in the company's financial strength
- Tend to be suspicious of new markets
- Prefer to apply the brakes (and should be encouraged to do so when appropriate)

Too much Protector, the company could stall. Too much Builder, the company could fail. Moving too slow or moving too fast makes managing more difficult and the top executive will struggle to gain buy-in.

The CEO must be a Builder and develop a like-minded team. However, the Protector mindset is helpful in small doses to counter the Builders' tendency toward over-inflated optimism.

> Too much Protector, the company could stall. Too much Builder, the company could fail.

DETERMINING YOUR COMPANY'S BUILDER/PROTECTOR RATIO

A leader can get a good idea of their company's Builder/Protector Ratio by:

1. Tuning into the voltage (think energy) in your company

2. Talking to the leadership team and asking pointed questions
3. Really listening to your employees

Get a read on your B/P Ratio by asking:

- Are people engaged in open and active dialogue?
- Are meetings productive and full of valuable information?
- Are good decisions being made?
- Does your leadership team and your employees appear optimistic about the future?
- Are they confident in the financial strength of the company?
- Do they have a high level of confidence in their co-workers?
- What are your employees saying?
- Is there behind-the-scenes gossiping?
- Is there a high rate of absenteeism or turnover?
- Do your managers or employees complain about a lack of accountability?
- Are projects often derailed or late?

If the company expands too fast and cash flow gets tight, you need to be the voice of caution. Pull back, rethink that next hire, or make a decision to expand the operation. Staying in the Protector mindset for too long isn't healthy for the organization, however.

You can move between the Builder/Protector mindset as the circumstances or situations require. Confidence needs to be continually balanced with a certain amount of caution. The team will take its cues from you and how you respond to challenges.

- -

WHAT IS TOO MUCH?

While the results of a Builder mindset tend to manifest in ways that help a company grow (drive sales, look for new opportunities, strong financials), too much of a Builder mindset can create issues; just as a prolonged Protector mindset can restrict growth.

SYMPTOMS OF TOO MUCH BUILDER:

1) Hockey stick sales projections

2) Hiring in advance of need

3) Taking on high-risk projects without proper reward

4) Over-committing and under-delivering

5) Lack of clarity in the direction of the company

SYMPTOMS OF TOO MUCH PROTECTOR:

1) Unwilling to try new marketing and business development techniques

2) Too much focus on expenses, not enough on revenue

3) Sees hurdles instead of opportunities

4) Insulated, not seeking divergent opinions

5) Fearful about the future

6) Lack of communication

7) Hesitant to embrace change

8) Decisions take too long and opportunities are missed

- -

Understanding your company's Builder/Protector Ratio improves your insight into your company's mental health by:

1. Measuring the company's ability to meet and overcome challenges.
2. Communicating the company's willingness to perceive and take advantage of opportunities in its path.
3. Measuring the strength of the company's immune defense system, acting as a barrier against low morale and poor performance.
4. Assessing the company's willingness to advance itself through change.
5. Gauging the company's belief in its future.
6. Communicating the company's trust in its leaders.

WHEN THE BUILDER/PROTECTOR RATIO IS OUT OF ALIGNMENT

The Builder/Protector Ratio for Stage 4 is 3:2. It's the only time there is a larger ratio of Protectors in the company. To understand why the ratio in Stage 4 is 3:2, we must look at the Stage 4 challenges. Four out of five challenges relate to process issues. The company is experiencing a huge increase in the number of processes required to manage the complexity. It is a time to slow the pace of change down a bit, focus on sustaining profitability and continue to improve performance.

The high Protector ratio is designed to counterbalance the impact of releasing more responsibility and authority to capable managers. With managers stepping into the day-to-day operations and the

CEO stepping away from some of those crucial areas, the need for a stronger Protector balance is critical. The CEO can't abdicate – she must delegate – and do so by setting strong expectations and managing to those expectations.

In the best-selling book by Rodd Wagner and James Harter, *12: The Elements of Great Managing*, the authors say, "One of the most fundamental needs of a great manager is ... a great manager." So, as a company moves into Stage 4, the CEO must assess her ability to become a role model for how she wants her company to be led.

I'll give you an example of how the Builder/Protector Ratio plays out in a Stage 4 enterprise. Widgets of the World, a product-based business, found itself struggling to maintain momentum when it left Stage 3.

ISSUES INCLUDED:

1. Fast growth with little time to train new people led to mistakes in the manufacturing process.
2. The CEO/founder knew the manufacturing process by heart but hadn't done a good job of capturing processes or identifying procedures. She was deeply involved in all aspects of delivering the product.
3. People with little management experience were put into management positions and expected to manage people and processes. The CEO/founder set unrealistic expectations with no follow up or accountability.
4. A widening gap between what the CEO/founder wanted and how the employees behaved.

5. Employees were afraid to identify flaws in the existing manufacturing process for fear of being reprimanded.

6. Managers were left to figure it out on their own, which caused the CEO/founder to step in and micromanage the manufacturing process.

7. Delivery dates were backlogged, forcing people to work overtime, causing mistakes and quality control issues that clients complained about.

8. Managers and employees experienced burnout and became frustrated with the lack of definitive processes to follow.

9. Profits eroded due to inattention to rising overhead costs without swift price adjustments.

What did this CEO do wrong? She overlooked her responsibility to hire and train exceptional managers. She thought that a good salary and a management title would lead to the desired results.

To create a strong Builder/Protector balance in Stage 4, a CEO has to have learned the art of delegation. In order for the company to scale, critical processes must be put in place and be managed by capable and experienced people. At the same time, a CEO must recognize the need to manage the managers. Anything less sets the company up for failure. When all decisions have to run through the CEO, managers feel second-guessed. The good ones will leave, creating more chaos.

Widgets of the World is a classic example of what happens when the Builder/Protector Ratio is out of whack. When the Ratio is out of alignment, the CEO sends a signal to the team that she is not confident about the direction of the company without even being aware of it. That lack of confidence manifests in key employees or the management team, and ultimately ricochets throughout the entire company.

Finding the right balance between a Builder and Protector mindset is key to surviving Stage 4. The CEO needs to provide strong direction, set expectations and manage to those expectations. The goal is to guide, manage, direct, coach, encourage and correct, which is how a CEO demonstrates a balance between confidence and caution.

A manager's engagement level ebbs and flows just as much as anyone else's. Managers want direction. They also want to be valued and feel that what they do every day has meaning. Once a CEO recognizes the role she plays in "managing the managers," the dynamic can change within weeks.

THE BUILDER/PROTECTOR RATIO FOR STAGE 1, STAGE 2, STAGE 3 AND STAGE 4

STAGE 1 (1 – 10 EMPLOYEES)	STAGE 2 (11 – 19 EMPLOYEES)	STAGE 3 (20 – 34 EMPLOYEES)	STAGE 4 (35 – 57 EMPLOYEES)
4:1	3:1	1:1	3:2

HIDDEN AGENT #2: THREE FACES OF A LEADER

The 7 Stages of Growth research uncovered the Three Faces of a Leader. The length of time a leader spends wearing one of these faces depends upon their stage of growth. There is a model percentage blend for each stage.

For a Stage 4 company, the Three Faces blend looks like this:

VISIONARY: 10%

Visionary leaders ensure the company knows where it wants to go. They can take the most insignificant situation and turn it into an opportunity. As the company begins to hire capable and experienced managers, keeping the vision in front of all employees becomes a bigger challenge. Part of a CEO's "Visionary Face" is to make sure the new managers are able to articulate the company's vision, mission and values.

Instead of "face time" between the CEO and the employees, they now report to and get direction from a manager. While that structure is exactly what a Stage 4 company needs, the CEO must recognize the importance of staying in touch with all of the employees.

Monthly meetings to connect with the staff and share the company vision and ideas for the future are critical for keeping employees engaged. With additional of layers of management and in the chaos of growth, employees can lose sight of the bigger picture and question why they are doing what they are doing.

Spend time talking with each employee about how they see the company and find out what they think the company's strengths and weaknesses are. Help them to see themselves in the future of the organization, and challenge them to continually grow and learn in order to help the company do the same.

MANAGER: 70%

The manager face understands the importance of growing a company through the management of workflow and people. A manager creates order and focuses on pragmatic systems and procedures that make the company run well. This requires emotional intelligence and dedication to helping people succeed.

The manager face has increased from 60% in Stage 3 to 70% in Stage 4—it's a critical lynchpin in running a successful Stage 4 company. As we learned in Stage 3, "Letting it go to let it grow" is all about surrounding yourself with people who are better at certain tasks and functions than you are.

The core question a Stage 4 leader must ask themselves is: How can I ensure that my employees will have great managers? Your job is to recruit, hire, train and develop skilled and experienced managers who know more about certain aspects of running your company than you do.

You're responsible for helping those new managers to emulate the company's culture by ensuring they are committed to growing their people, providing exceptional customer service and protecting the company's financial assets – all elements that were once part of your role as a Builder.

Most of us are familiar with Gallup's surveys on employee engagement. The 2017 State of the Workforce Report was less than encouraging.

"In the U.S., only 33% of employees are engaged in their job. Slightly more than half of employees (51%) say they are actively looking for a new job or watching for openings, and 35% of worker's report changing jobs within the past three years. Workers want to feel connected to their job, manager and company. If those ties are not there, they have all the more incentive to quit, leaving their organization to start the costly recruitment, hiring and onboarding dance all over again."

The business graveyard is full of companies that pretended to believe "their people are their greatest asset." Sadly, the catchphrase is rarely attached to any actions or practices that back it up.

SPECIALIST: 20%

The specialist face represents the work the company produces. Specialists understand the need to capture the necessary processes, to deliver the work and meet clients' needs. In most cases, the specialist is the person who came up with the idea to start the company; she is action oriented and detail focused.

In Stage 3, it was important to help employees gain ownership of the roles in delivering the product or service to customers. With 35 – 57 employees, the needs shift. The CEO should only spend 20% of her time on product or service development and distribution. With capable managers in place to handle different aspects of product or service, the CEO will need to focus on managing the managers.

Don't misunderstand. No one knows the product or service better than the founder. To ignore or distance yourself too far from the product or service is not smart. The message is simply to re-focus on helping the managers become the experts.

THREE FACES OF A LEADER FOR STAGE 1, STAGE 2 AND STAGE 3

STAGE 1 (1 – 10 EMPLOYEES)	
VISIONARY	40%
MANAGER	10%
SPECIALIST	50%

STAGE 2 (11 – 19 EMPLOYEES)	
VISIONARY	40%
MANAGER	20%
SPECIALIST	40%

STAGE 3 (20 – 34 EMPLOYEES)	
VISIONARY	10%
MANAGER	60%
SPECIALIST	30%

STAGE 4 (35 - 57 EMPLOYEES)	
VISIONARY	10%
MANAGER	70%
SPECIALIST	20%

THE THREE FACES AT WORK

A CEO of a growing company needs to bring all three faces (Visionary, Manager and Specialist) to the table every day. The three faces provide the much-needed focus to clarify roles and responsibilities for each and every position. Hire capable managers to identify capable employees who can take on more responsibility and help everyone in the organization become confident in their abilities.

You'll also need to focus on the financial side of your business. Make sure you have a profit plan in place, are monitoring cash flow weekly and have established key indicators for all aspects of the company. The ability to handle critical conversations and not let poor performance go unnoticed is important. Follow up and verify that what needs to be done is being done to your satisfaction.

A CEO who believes that employees come to the table to succeed and embraces her role as a manager in Stage 4 will successfully navigate their growth curve. Take the time to focus on the needs of your people. Ask people for their insight and ideas before providing answers. Find out what their goals and dreams are. Remember, your people ARE your business. Understanding how to manage them is essential.

HIDDEN AGENT #3: LEADERSHIP STYLE

Leaders create resonance in an organization by ensuring the entire fabric of a company is laced with emotional intelligence. Developing a new leadership style means changing how one operates with other people.

What do winning leaders have in common?

- They are aware of their own emotions and attuned with empathy toward the people they lead.
- They understand that handling relationships well begins with authenticity.

If a leader acts disingenuously or manipulatively, for instance, their team will immediately sense a note of falseness, which leads to distrust. The ability to connect emotionally to the people you lead is important for an environment that fosters involvement and commitment from everyone in your company.

KEY LEADERSHIP STYLES

The six Leadership Styles from Daniel Goleman's incredibly useful book, *Primal Leadership: Unleashing the Power of Emotional Intelligence* are summarized here for your reference.

1. **Visionary:** Visionary leaders frame the collective task in terms of a grander vision. Employees are encouraged to innovate and work toward shared goals that build team commitment. People are proud to belong to the organization.

2. **Coaching:** Coaching leaders communicate a belief in people's potential and an expectation they will do their best. By linking people's daily work to long-term goals, coaches keep people motivated.

3. **Affiliative:** Affiliative leaders recognize employees as people and put less emphasis on accomplishing tasks and goals. Such leaders build tremendous loyalty and strengthen connectedness.

4. **Democratic:** A democratic leader builds on a triad of primal leadership abilities: teamwork and collaboration, conflict management and influence. Listening is the key strength of this "team member" leadership style.

5. **Pacesetting:** A pacesetter leader holds and exemplifies high standards for performance. The primal leadership foundation of this style lies in the drive to achieve by continually finding ways to improve their own performance and that of those they lead.

6. **Commanding:** Commanding leaders draw on three primal leadership competencies: influence, achievement and initiative. They exert forceful direction to get better results and opportunities are seized in an unhesitating tone.

Great leaders move us. They ignite our passion and inspire the best in us. When people try to explain great leadership, they talk about vision, strategy and powerful ideas. The reality is great leadership works through emotions. It's *how* you connect to people that leads to success.

Your job as a leader just got harder or easier, depending on how you want to look at it. You have the power to sway everyone's emotions. If you push people with enthusiasm and open communication, performance will soar. If you drive them with rancor and anxiety, they will return in kind.

The reason a leader's manner – not just *what* she does but *how* she does it – matters so much lies in the design of the human brain: what scientist have started

> If you push people with enthusiasm and open communication, performance will soar.

to call the "open loop" of our emotional centers. A closed loop system, such as the circulatory system, is self-regulating. What's happening in the circulatory system of those around us does not impact our own system. An open loop system depends largely on external sources to manage itself.

In other words, we rely on connections with other people for our own emotional stability. In intensive care units, research has shown that the comforting presence of another person not only lowers the patient's blood pressure, but also slows the secretion of fatty acids that block arteries.

Here's a startling statistic: three or more incidents of intense stress within a year (financial trouble, being fired or a divorce) triple the death rate in socially isolated, middle aged men. Alternatively, incidents of stress have zero impact on the death rate of men who cultivate close relationships.

This open loop system says "people need people." The ability of a leader to connect to their people at work can have the same healthy results as when that emotional awareness is taken home.

STYLES NEED TO BE PRACTICED AND ADJUSTED

Leadership is a skill like any other. Anyone who has the will and the motivation can become a better leader. Understanding the steps and taking the time to practice can turn a mediocre leader into one who inspires greatness. Improvement starts with understanding where you are today and what you aspire to be. That's why a solid diagnosis of your leadership strengths and weaknesses and a plan for development are crucial. Tuned-out, dissonant leaders are one of the main reasons that talented people leave a company, taking precious knowledge with them.

Our guiding values are represented in the pre-frontal areas of the brain as a hierarchy; what we love is at the top and what we loathe is at the bottom. What keeps us moving toward our goals comes down to the mind's ability to remind us how satisfied we will feel when we accomplish them.

What does this mean to you as a leader? Wherever people gravitate within their work role indicates where their real pleasure lies. That pleasure is itself motivating. External motivations don't get people to perform at their absolute best–it's an inside job!

Why should you care? By tuning into the desires, dreams and career goals of your employees, you gain insight into what motivates them. If you can take their passion and turn it into a driving force in their jobs, you've started to build a company that can truly go from being good to great.

To succeed, leadership development must be the strategic priority of the enterprise. Understanding the six leadership styles and how they impact each stage of growth is a powerful tool for any CEO. In the 7 Stages of Growth model, there are three critical leadership styles for each stage of growth. They are stacked in order of importance.

The top leadership styles for a Stage 4 leader are Coaching, Affiliative and Pacesetting. A successful leader must be able to bring all three styles into play based on the situation, but in Stage 4, Coaching is the most effective style.

> **Leadership development must be the strategic priority of the enterprise.**

WHAT DOES A COACHING STYLE LOOK LIKE?

When you utilize a Coaching style, your role is to connect an individual's goals with the company's goals. Coaching leaders motivate and enhance employee performance by building long-term capabilities and self-confidence. While Coaching is the most effective style, it is also the least used. Patience and a willingness to learn the art of delegation are required and too often, leaders feel the need to solve instead of teach or listen.

This story from *Primal Leadership*, by Daniel Goleman, illustrates how effective a Coaching style can be.

She was new at the firm and eight months pregnant. Staying late one night, she looked up from her work and was startled to see her boss standing at her door. He asked how she was doing, sat down, and started talking with her. He wanted to know all about her life. How did she like her job? Where did she want to go in her career? Would she come back to work after she had the baby?

These conversations continued daily over the next month until the woman had her baby. The boss was David Ogilvy, the legendary advertising executive. The pregnant newcomer was Shelley Lazarus, now CEO of Ogilvy & Mather, the huge ad agency that Ogilvy founded. One of the main reasons Lazarus says she's still here, decades later, is the bond she forged with mentor Ogilvy in those first after-hour conversations.

Today, Shelley Lazarus is Chairman Emeritus of Ogilvy & Mather. Her love for the company she helped to build and for the man who taught her what running a business is all about is strong to this day.

> Of all the things we talked about, I remember most what he said about people. He said to me: "You can never spend too much time thinking about, worrying about and caring about your people because, at the end of the day, it's only the people who matter. Nothing else. If you always hire people who are smaller than you are, we shall become a company of dwarfs. If, on the other hand, you always hire people who are bigger than you are, we shall become a company of giants."

Coaching leaders not only retain talented people, they build an organization that encourages accountability and transparency. A leader who uses the Coaching style helps employees uncover answers and solutions, identify their unique strengths and weaknesses, and ties those attributes to their personal and career aspirations. They help employees conceptualize a plan for reaching goals, while being specific about their own responsibility as well at the employees. Coaching isn't hand holding, it's giving someone a hand.

Larry Bossidy, co-author of *Execution: The Art of Getting Things Done*, believes good coaching is about trying to impart experience. In his article, "The Art of Good Coaching," he says, "You try to point out the best way of doing something, not because you are so smart, but because you've seen

Coaching isn't hand holding, it's giving someone a hand.

it 100 times." Bossidy believes that if he helps people find a better way of doing something, he's contributing to their overall success, which is what coaching is all about. Conversely, if your people don't get better, it's your fault too. The article goes on to say, "Coaching and performance are intricately tied." You can get short-term performance by dictating what needs to be done or you can create an environment where people are continually coached to deliver great performance.

Coaching is a two-way street. You need to listen to how people respond. A good coach has great interpersonal skills, is a good communicator and knows when to press and when to praise. They show people how their participation fits into the overall goals of the company.

A Coaching leader is good at delegating and gives employees goals that stretch them, not just tasks that get a job done. Coaching works best with employees who show initiative and are looking for opportunities to improve. A surprisingly positive emotional impact stems from the leader's willingness to communicate a belief in people's potential. Leaders who have a high degree of empathy, who listen first before reacting or giving feedback, often ask themselves, "Is this about my issue or goal, or theirs?"

In Simon Synek's book, *Start With Why*, he talks about how most companies understand *what* they do. They make sure they have a value proposition that describes *how* they do it, but the challenge for many organizations is helping people understand the *why*. In Synek's research great leader's work from the inside out. They start with the *why* and make sure every single person in the company understands that *why* too. The Coaching style supports this "inside out" approach, which is why this style is the most effective tool a leader can bring to their organization.

WHAT DOES AN AFFILIATIVE STYLE LOOK LIKE?

Called the "relationship builder," the Affiliative style represents collaborative competence in action. Affiliative leaders are primarily concerned with promoting harmony and fostering friendly interactions between the people they lead. This style shows up in Stage 4, Stage 5 and Stage 6. The leader must recognize the importance of building relationships with the people they have put their trust in to run the business. Affiliative leaders tend to care more about the people they manage than the actual act of getting tasks done. The reason? They have capable people to do those tasks, which gives them the time and focus to promote the company's culture, work on developing strong leaders and stay on top of how the company is running.

Affiliative leaders focus on their employee's emotional needs and make empathy – the ability to sense the feelings, needs, and perspectives of others – a critical competence. When the Affiliative leadership style is combined with empathy, a CEO has the ability to lift her employees' spirits even when they trudge through mundane tasks.

However, leaders who tend to be overly nice or worry too much about building harmony can create problems. An obvious flaw that can occur when a leader relies too heavily on the affiliative approach is that work takes a second place to feelings. When this style is overused, corrective feedback on performance suffers or opportunities to help employees improve are ignored.

According to Goleman in *Primal Leadership*, "This anxious type of affiliation has been found to drive down climate rather than raise it. Stewing about where they're liked or not, such leaders' avoidance of confrontation can derail a group, steering them to failure." In Stage 4, when a leader must delegate authority and responsibility, too much reliance on this style leaves new managers looking for direction and constructive advice. If the Affiliative leader is too busy being nice, the company will spin out of control.

All six of the leadership styles used in the 7 Stages of Growth are most effective when used in conjunction with other styles and competencies. The Affiliative style combined with the Coaching style produces the best results.

WHAT DOES A PACESETTING STYLE LOOK LIKE?

The Pacesetting style focuses on high performance. It can look like micromanaging, because there is an emphasis on immediate, short-term goals, such as sales numbers.

Used sparingly, this style can help set the standard for excellence, especially if the leader exemplifies that excellence in their actions, not just their words. According to Goleman, "Pacesetting makes sense in particular during the entrepreneurial phase of a company's life cycle, when growth is all important." When a team is highly competent, motivated and needs little direction, this style can be effective.

The challenge for a Pacesetting leader is to know when to back off. Pacesetters tend to be unclear about setting expectations and establishing guidelines. They are results-focused and can come off as uncaring, which causes employees to feel they are being pushed too hard or worse, that the leader doesn't trust them. The more pressure they put on people for results, the more anxiety it provokes. Morale can plummet under a strict Pacesetting leader and poor performance will become the norm. When people lose sight of the vision, the exceptional employees will leave.

This style needs to be balanced with the Coaching and Affiliative styles, so people remain motivated and feel the leader cares about their success. To achieve sustainable growth, expectations must be defined and managed. Pacesetting leaders must continually find ways to improve performance, which means seizing opportunities. When leaders show initiative combined with goal setting, Pacesetting becomes a strength and not a weakness.

LEADERSHIP STYLES FOR STAGE 1, STAGE 2, STAGE 3 AND STAGE 4

STAGE 1 (1-10 EMPLOYEES)	STAGE 2 (11 – 19 EMPLOYEES)	STAGE 3 (20 – 34 EMPLOYEES)	STAGE 4 (35 – 57 EMPLOYEES)
VISIONARY	COACHING	COACHING	COACHING
COACHING	PACESETTING	DEMOCRATIC	AFFILIATIVE
COMMANDING	COMMANDING	PACESETTING	PACESETTING

WHEN LEADERSHIP STYLE IS OUT OF ALIGNMENT

The ability to effectively utilize all six leadership styles is what distinguishes an emotionally aware leader from a leader who elects to focus more on tasks than people. Business owners feel a tremendous sense of urgency when launching a new product or service.

The pressure forces the leader to be more direct and there can be a tendency to micro-manage in the early stages of growth. A Pacesetting or Commanding style may work in the short term but not in the long term.

When a company moves into Stage 4 and needs to focus on how to encourage people to take on new and different roles and responsibilities, the ability to listen and teach, not direct, is critical. A leader who is unable or unwilling to release control will send a negative message to capable employees, causing those employees to question their value and their roles. Just when that leader needs to rely on others, her own inability to adjust her leadership style to the needs of the company can derail growth and undermine trust. When leaders hide behind their own failings, good companies become poisonous environments and very rarely recover.

Developing a new leadership style means learning to change how you operate with people. The first step in this journey is to honestly assess your effectiveness today. Leadership development isn't a program; it's a strategic initiative that needs to permeate a culture and encourage personal development, starting at the top. By understanding all six of the leadership styles and adjusting their leadership style to each stage of growth, a CEO will be better prepared for the changes that come as the company adds employees.

> Leadership development isn't a program; it's a strategic initiative.

Take the Leadership Style Assessment to identify your strengths and weaknesses.

LEADERSHIP STYLE ASSESSMENT

Directions: Within each grouping of six statements please select the statement that most represents your leadership style and put the #6 after it. Then select your second choice by assigning it a #5. Then select your third choice by assigning it a #4 and so on until you select your last choice by assigning it a # 1.

A. Your leadership style helps the organization understand where it is going. _____

B. Your leadership style helps people identify their unique strengths and weaknesses and tying those to personal and career aspirations. _____

C. Your leadership style helps people repair broken trust in the organization._____

D. Your leadership style is based on genuinely listening to people. _____

E. Your leadership style is based on a high standard of excellence. _____

F. Your leadership style is based on a decisive commanding presence that people can trust. _____

A. People feel pride in the organization as a result of your values and vision. _____

B. People believe that your advice is genuinely in their best interest. _____

C. People experience greater harmony, better communication and improved morale based on your leadership abilities. _____

D. People believe that you can settle any conflict. _____

E. People feel a drive to improve their performance in your company. _____

F. People under your leadership have clear guidelines and understand what is expected of them. _____

A. As a result of your leadership style people see how their work fits into the big picture. _____

B. As a result of your leadership style people have a sense that you believe in them and that you expect their very best effort. _____

C. As a result of your leadership style people feel they are more important to you than the task they are doing. _____

D. As a result of your leadership style people believe they are really a part of an overall team. _____

E. As a result of your leadership style people feel a need to create new opportunities for the company. _____

YOUR TOP LEADERSHIP STYLE

Thanks for taking the Leadership Styles Assessment. Once you have captured your scores and placed them in the appropriate area below, look at the 'key' section to determine what your top leadership style is based on where you are today. Remember, leadership styles are situational. The value in identifying your leadership style and comparing it with where you are in your stage of growth is to help you understand if your leadership style is a hidden agent that may be hindering your ability to help your company grow.

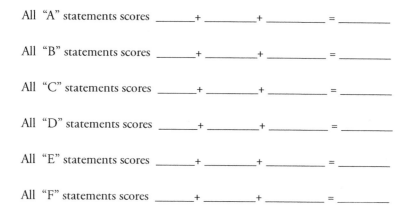

All "A" statements scores _____ + _____ + _____ = _____

All "B" statements scores _____ + _____ + _____ = _____

All "C" statements scores _____ + _____ + _____ = _____

All "D" statements scores _____ + _____ + _____ = _____

All "E" statements scores _____ + _____ + _____ = _____

All "F" statements scores _____ + _____ + _____ = _____

THE KEY TO YOUR LEADERSHIP STYLES:

A score = Visionary: The Visionary Leader is particularly effective when changes, even a business turnaround, require a new vision or clarifying a new direction. People are motivated by Visionary Leadership toward shared dreams that resonate with a company's values, goals and mission.

B score = Coaching: The Coaching Leader connects what a person wants with the company's goals. A good Coaching Leader motivates and enhances employee performance by building long-term capabilities and self-confidence. It is by getting to know their employees on a deeper, personal level that these leaders make that link a reality.

C score = Affiliative: An Affiliative Leader creates harmony by connecting people to each other, often healing rifts in a team, providing motivation during stressful times or strengthening connections. The focus is on the emotional needs of employees over works goals. This empathy allows a leader to care for the whole person and boosts morale par excellence.

D score = Democratic: A Democratic Leader values people's input and they get commitments through participation. They typically are attuned to a wide range of people and they build consensus when unclear about which direction to take. This often generates fresh ideas for executing it.

E score = Pacesetting: Pacesetting Leaders meet challenging and exciting goals to get high-quality results from a motivated and competent team. These leaders require initiative and the hyper-vigilant readiness to create opportunities to do better and meet goals. This leadership style's continual high pressure performance zone can be debilitating for employees. These leaders typically lack self-awareness or the ability to collaborate or communicate effectively hence employee morale plummets and a total lack of trust ensues.

F score = Commanding: In a crisis, this leadership style can kick-start a turn-around and allay fears by providing crystal clear direction. A Commanding Leader is highly successful at unfreezing useless business habits or ruts and they relentlessly drive for better results. A legacy of the old command-and-control hierarchies that typified 20th century businesses, this military approach is truly appropriate to the battlefield, hospital emergency room or a hostile takeover.

Largest number is your dominant style. Second largest number is your secondary style. Third largest number is your auxiliary style. In case of a tie, you need to declare a preference between the styles. Based on the work of Daniel Goleman, Richard Boyatzis and Annie McKee, Primal Leadership, Harvard Universit.

HIDDEN AGENT #4: NON-NEGOTIABLE LEADERSHIP RULES

Getting focused on the right things at the right time spells success for any leader of a growing organization. Getting an entire team of people focused on the right things at the right time is what takes good companies and makes them great.

The 7 Stages of Growth research has provided us with rules of the road that help business owners focus on critical aspects of their company as they move through the different stages of growth. Each stage of growth offers 5 Non-Negotiable Leadership Rules that give business owner's specific guidelines on what they need to take seriously in terms of activities designed to create a solid foundation on which to grow.

As the President of a company that grew beyond my expectations, I struggled to find ways to engage employees in understanding what was needed to manage that growth. However, once I began to understand the stages of growth and could articulate the rules of the road, that challenge became easier to manage. Why? Because I was talking a language each employee in my company could understand.

Growing a business demands every minute of your energy, resources and brainpower. The good news is you don't have to reinvent the wheel. By understanding your stage of growth, by knowing what the rules of the road are for each stage of growth, you will have headlights to help you navigate the curves and get ahead of the obstacles. One thing we have learned is that "What you don't get done in your current stage of growth will simply not just go away." The rules in each stage of growth need to be addressed and if they aren't, you will face them again as you move to the next stage of growth.

As you read through the rules of the road for a Stage 1 – Stage 4 company, you'll have tools you can use to help your entire company begin to understand what is needed from everyone to succeed.

STAGE 1 LEADERSHIP RULES OF THE ROAD – 1 – 10 EMPLOYEES:

RULE #1:
GENERATE, TRACK AND PRESERVE CASH.

Do you receive a daily report that tells you how you are doing on your company key indicators?

Do you have a simple budget and a 6 – 8 week rolling cash flow system to help you manage your company's cash?

Are you focused on getting new customers and increasing the transaction value and the frequency of those transactions to build your top line revenue?

RULE #2:
FOCUS 80% OF YOUR RESOURCES ON SELLING THE 2 – 3 OFFERINGS WITH THE BEST MARGINS.

Are you focusing 80% of your marketing, sales and customer service resources on your 3 top offerings?

Are you tracking your production output?

Do you know what your cost of goods and gross margins are on your products and service offerings sold?

RULE #3:

HIRE FIRST FOR HOW THE PERSON FITS IN WITH THE TEAM AND SECOND FOR HOW COMPETENT THEY ARE.

Do you have a clear profile of the criteria that makes a good company fit?

Do you have clearly defined roles and responsibilities for all staff positions?

Do you have a standard interview process that you use to screen new job applicants?

RULE #4:

EMBRACE CHAOS – COMMAND THE TEAM AND INSPIRE THE EMPLOYEES.

Do you consistently set the company's priorities and clearly communicate them to your staff?

Have you clearly articulated the company's vision for the future and regularly communicate it to your staff?

Have you insured that your team has a clear mission, a clear set of instructions and practical goals to reach?

RULE #5:

ESTABLISH A PERFORMANCE MINDSET, A COMMUNICATION FEEDBACK LOOP AND EMPLOYEE DEVELOPMENT PROGRAM.

Have you established clear performance expectations with every employee?

Do you have an employee skill development program in place?

Do you consistently gather and give feedback to your employees?

STAGE 2 LEADERSHIP RULES OF THE ROAD – 11 - 19 EMPLOYEES:

RULE #1:
SELL ABSOLUTELY EVERY DAY.

Do you organize your schedule to sell every day?

Have you set up an effective sales process?

Do you have a contact management system in place to effectively follow up with leads, prospects and clients?

RULE #2:
DEVELOP, WITHOUT FAIL, THREE EMPLOYEE LEADERS TO BE RESPONSIBLE, ACCOUNTABLE AND PROACTIVE.

Have you defined clear roles of responsibility with three supervisor candidates?

Do you meet weekly one-on-one with these supervisors to support their commitment to performance-based goals?

Do you reward these key supervisors when they proactively demonstrate signs of leadership?

RULE #3:
CREATE A DAILY, WEEKLY AND MONTHLY KEY INDICATOR INSTRUMENT PANEL/FLASH SHEET.

Have you determined key health indicators for each department in your company?

Have you organized a system to engage the daily collection of key health indicator data from staff?

Have you formulated a daily, weekly and monthly flash sheet system report you can review regularly?

RULE #4:
COMMUNICATE ANY AND ALL DIRECTIONS IN WRITING.

Have you set up a simple CEO memo system template when communicating with staff that sets priority level of tasks, purpose, objectives and directions?

Do you have a retrieval system for all written memo directions?

Do you use the written memos during work performance reviews?

RULE #5:
DRIVE SMALL ACTION TEAMS TO HIT GOALS.

Do you set clear and agreed upon action team goals?

Do you organize and facilitate crisp action team meetings?

Do you organize/review regular team action lists and delegate tasks and due dates?

STAGE 3 LEADERSHIP RULES OF THE ROAD – 20 - 34 EMPLOYEES:

RULE #1:
DELEGATE RESPONSIBILITY AND AUTHORITY TO CAPABLE SUPERVISORS AND MEET WITH THEM REGULARLY.

Have you appointed a supervisory team and do you meet with them weekly?

At these meetings, do you delegate, track and review specific authority and responsibility to each supervisor?

Have you identified and developed a company-wide daily key indicator system?

RULE #2:
CREATE A FINANCIAL REPORTING AND PROJECTION SYSTEM.

Have you organized your profit and loss statement based on revenue groups?

Have you developed a weekly cash flow report?

Do you have a profit plan and are you reviewing it monthly with key employees?

RULE #3:
INSTILL A TEAM-BASED MINDSET THROUGHOUT THE COMPANY.

Have you created a team credo?

Have you outlined clear roles and responsibilities for all team members?

Have you identified the values that will drive behavior and instill accountability?

RULE #4:
OVERHAUL THE BUSINESS MODEL.

Recently, have you challenged all assumptions regarding vision, mission, goals, objectives and strategies of the company?

Do you regularly challenge all assumptions about the customer, the competition, the market and your company's offerings?

Are you focused on reorganizing the company's resources to meet the new business design conclusions?

RULE #5:
WITHOUT FAIL, CLARIFY AND STRENGTHEN
ANY AND ALL COMMUNICATION
WITH YOUR EMPLOYEES.

Do you clearly communicate the goals and direction of the company to all employees?

Have you established and demonstrated the company's core guiding values, preferably with input from your employees?

Are you consistently meeting one-on-one with direct reports each week?

STAGE 4 LEADERSHIP RULES OF THE ROAD – 35 - 57 EMPLOYEES:

RULE #1:
HIRE AND EFFECTIVELY TRAIN PROFESSIONAL DEPARTMENT MANAGERS WHO ARE RESPONSIBLE, ACCOUNTABLE AND PROACTIVE.

Have you defined clear roles and responsibilities for all department manager positions?

Do you meet weekly to support department manager's commitment to reach their goals?

Do you reward managers when they demonstrate proactive signs of leadership?

RULE #2:
CREATE STRONG, HIGH-PERFORMING DEPARTMENTS THAT ARE CONFIDENT, CAPABLE AND ABLE TO SERVE INTERNAL AND EXTERNAL CUSTOMERS.

Has each department established clear, measurable goals and objectives that show up in performance reviews?

Do your departments hold weekly meetings centered around key health indicators?

Do all managers establish, get approved and manage their department's budget?

RULE #3:
ALLOCATE 5% – 10% OF GROSS REVENUES TO IDENTIFY, ACQUIRE AND IMPLEMENT NEW SYSTEMS.

Do you and/or your team identify key systems required to sustain enterprise health and improved performance?

Have you established research practices that help you acquire key systems?

Do you have a plan in place to organize and execute the implementation of those key systems?

RULE #4:
IDENTIFY AND SET IN PLACE THE COMPANY'S CORE MASTER PROCESSES WITH THE MANAGEMENT TEAM.

Have you identified the top 10 to 15 master processes needed to create and sustain the company's health?

Is there a plan in place to design, document and refine those top 10 to 15 master processes?

Do you understand the importance of implementing and making the necessary improvements to the top 10 to 15 master processes?

RULE #5:
ESTABLISH A STRICT PROJECT MANAGEMENT TEMPLATE.

Have you done the research and designed a clear, consistent process to manage internal projects?

Is there a process in place to train all management staff on the project management template?

Are you focused on communicating and training all staff on the company's project management template?

These rules of the road will fundamentally drive your business to succeed. By keying in on these critical elements for your current stage of growth, you'll begin to proactively manage your growth, instead of letting growth manage you.

Spend time answering each question under each rule – don't gloss over them thinking they don't affect you. You don't have to reinvent how to manage growth. By spending time every day on these rules of the road you'll watch productivity increase and profits grow.

HIDDEN AGENT #5: LEADERSHIP COMPETENCIES

Growth, Integrity, Fun, Collaboration, Excellence – these were the values we embraced at the marketing communications company I helped grow from two to over 100 employees. Leaving that company after 14 years was a very difficult decision. The reasons were personal. My husband's daughter, my step-daughter, committed suicide at 20. Our world was rocked to its core. It was my choice to leave the company I loved and spend time helping us both heal.

I loved working with our staff. I loved mentoring, coaching, teaching, supporting and yes, I even grew to appreciate having those hard conversations because I was committed to making our company a great place for people to work. I made it a point to try to connect with every employee, every day. I sent out birthday cards, I asked about their challenges, their successes. This wasn't hard for me. It was who I was. However, as a leader in a fast-growing organization, I spent a lot of time putting out fires, dealing with crisis, managing projects, managing people, and managing financials. I never really stopped to think about the kind of leader I was.

My last day at the company was a celebration. I loved the turnout – clients traveled from out of state to attend, most of our current employees were there and even more amazing, people who had left the company and moved on showed up to say their goodbyes. As bitter sweet as that day was, the small 4" x 4" journal full of personal sentiments, memories and photos of my years at this remarkable company is something I treasure to this day.

Leadership is a lonely journey. You have to make decisions every day that impact people, processes and profit and you seldom get the luxury of celebrating the ones that go well. Remembering the ones that didn't go well, on the other hand, keep us up at night.

I share some of the excerpts from my going away journal – not to brag or pat myself on the back – but to remind myself and others that as leaders that our impact is felt, every day. This is particularly true when we are true to our own values and believe that people are the most important asset of a company.

This from Patrick:

LT – Five years ago, on my 50ᵗʰ birthday, you sent me these words on a card. I'm sending them back to you because they apply to you, too. You wrote: "I so value your creativity, your insight, your ability to understand and absorb critical information. All those skills have really helped set us apart from the competition."

Or this from Christy:

"Laurie – you have been an exceptional leader. Thank you for constantly inspiring us to be our best. And thank you for allowing us the room to grow and offering your full-hearted support."

And Maia wrote:

"Thanks for the birthday cards, your open door and thanks for helping build a company I've loved working for."

Lorie, a new employee, wrote:

"You gave me the fuel to jump right in and start digging. You mentored me, counseled me and on one occasion when I was feeling overwhelmed, you looked me straight in the eye and said: 'Lorie you can do this!' That conviction, that honesty, that energy – that is a true work of leadership art, that is Laurie Taylor."

One more quote that touched my heart said:

"It's been a pleasure to work with you, gain inspiration from you, and learn how to do everything better simply by watching you."

As a leader, responsible for your employees, never take your influence for granted. Never assume no one is listening or paying attention. Great leaders move us. They ignite passion and inspire the best in us. Know that every "hello" you offer, every birthday you remember, every success you help someone celebrate, and yes, every difficult conversation that tells someone you care about how they are doing, is remembered. Your leadership competencies are put to the test every day. They are worth understanding and the outcomes they deliver help shape the culture of the organization you lead.

> As a leader, responsible for your employees, never take your influence for granted.

At each stage of growth, a leader is directed to focus on five critical competencies. The 7 Stages of Growth model helps CEOs focus on the "right things at the right time." Becoming adept at 18 critical competencies overnight can be overwhelming. As a CEO navigates her company through the different stages, she should be aware of which competencies are necessary to develop, based on the current stage of growth.

A quote from the book, *Primal Leadership*, says: "No creature can fly with just one wing. Gifted leadership occurs where heart and head – feeling and thought – meet. These are the two wings that allow a leader to soar."

EMOTIONAL INTELLIGENCE DOMAINS AND ASSOCIATED COMPETENCIES FOR A STAGE 4 LEADER

Of Daniel Goleman's 18 Leadership Competencies, five of them are critical for Stage 4 leaders, specifically.

1. **Adaptability** – Flexibility in adapting to changing situations or overcoming obstacles. Leaders who are adaptable can manage the challenge of multiple demands without losing focus or energy. They are nimble in adjusting to change and comfortable with the ambiguities that come with running a growing company.

This competency falls under the Leadership Competency domain of *Self-Management*: the focused drive that all leaders need to achieve their goals. If we don't know what we are feeling, we are at a loss as to how to manage those feelings. We tend to let our emotions control us. Emotions are a strength when it comes to creating the positive, good feelings that come from meeting a challenge or enthusiasm overall. There's no room for negative emotions in the workplace, such as frustration, rage, anxiety or panic.

Self-Management is an emotional intelligence tool that frees us from being a prisoner of our feelings. Because leadership demands mental clarity and high energy, it's easy for our emotions to throw us off track. Leaders who master the competencies that fall under Self-Management embody "an upbeat, optimistic enthusiasm" that resonates throughout our organizations.

Adaptability shows up as a necessary competency in Stage 4 because of the changes a leader must undergo when she hires capable and competent managers. The company is much more complex; effective processes must be introduced and supported. The CEO needs to model how managers should manage in order to maintain employee engagement. Overcoming obstacles? Being flexible? Never has it been more important for a leader to embrace Adaptability.

2. **Organizational Awareness**: Reading the currents, decision networks and politics at the organizational level. A leader strong in this competency can understand the values and unspoken rules that guide behaviors.

3. **Service:** Recognizing and meeting follower, client or customer needs. A leader who understands

the value of this competency fosters an emotional climate that helps people focus on the critical relationships that exist with customers and co-workers. She ensures everyone connected to the organization gets what they need, when they need it.

These two competencies are from the Leadership Competency domain of *Social Awareness*. Social awareness is critical for the leader to drive resonance, a sense of shared values and set priorities; all of which are necessary for team engagement.

One of the most important competencies under Social Awareness is Empathy, a competency that shows up in Stage 1 and again in Stage 2, reminding a leader that this competency can't be ignored. Organizational awareness and service will be difficult to apply without understanding the impact that empathy has on interactions with others.

Competencies require awareness – what they are, why they are important – and practice. Someone who is not empathic cannot acquire this critical competency overnight. They can learn how to be more empathetic by recognizing the importance of reading other people's emotions. A CEO who finds herself in Stage 4 with up to 57 employees, who has little or no desire to manage people, will appear disingenuous or manipulative if she isn't willing to learn the value of relationship management skills.

Because a Stage 4 leader is more removed from the rest of the company, due to the addition of managers, it's easy to lose touch with decision networks, to misinterpret culture currents and to make assumptions that aren't based on facts. Too often, Stage 4 leaders lose sight of who her customers are and rely on managers to stay in touch with key customers. The wake-up call for a leader in Stage 4 can come too late if she allows herself to stray too far from either employees or customers. Having a competency in Service will help that leader maintain critical connections.

4. **Developing Others:** Bolstering others' abilities through feedback and guidance. When leaders are adept at this competency, they show genuine interest in helping others succeed by understanding their goals, aspirations, strengths and weaknesses.

5. **Teamwork and Collaboration:** A leader's ability to draw people into active, enthusiastic commitment to the collective effort ensures an atmosphere of collegiality and team-ness. This leadership competency is at the heart of a company that values employees and is focused on forging and cementing relationships.

These two competencies fall under the Leadership Competency domain of Relationship Management. This is where we find the most visible tools of leadership: persuasion, conflict management, and collaboration among them. The ability to skillfully manage relationships boils down to handling other people's emotions. Leaders must be aware of their own emotions and attuned to the people they lead.

By Stage 4, someone in the organization needs to be skilled at developing others and focused on building a culture of teamwork and collaboration.

However, leaders can't be all things to all people. My business partner was a change catalyst. While adept at influencing others, dealing with conflict and being transparent, she wasn't terribly empathetic. We balanced each other well because I brought the competencies to the organization she lacked: empathy, developing others, teamwork, collaboration and inspirational leadership. Knowing what to look for in a business partner or an employee can help a business round out the skills needed to grow a successful business.

Being aware of which of the 18 competencies you feel are your strengths and which ones you aren't as confident about, is a great exercise. Then just compare your strengths and weaknesses with which competencies serve you best for your current stage of growth. By identifying areas that you might need to improve based on your stage of growth, you may uncover an area that if you spent time improving, could remove an obstacle to growth.

LEADERSHIP COMPETENCY ASSESSMENT

Directions: Please go through the following list of leadership competencies and chose the five most important leadership competencies that you have developed by marking the word TOP after each one. Then please go through the list again and chose the five competencies that are your least developed by marking the word LEAST after each choice.

SELF AWARENESS

1. Emotional self awareness: Reading one's own emotions and recognizing their impact on others _____
2. Accurate self assessment: Knowing one's strengths and limits _____
3. Self confidence: Having a sound sense of one's self worth and capabilities _____

SELF MANAGEMENT

4. Emotional self control: Keeping disruptive emotions and impulses under control _____
5. Transparency: Displaying honesty and integrity: trustworthiness _____
6. Adaptability: Flexibility in adapting to changing situations or overcoming obstacles _____
7. Achievement: The drive to improve performance to meet inner standards of excellence _____
8. Initiative: Readiness to act and seize opportunities _____
9. Optimism: Seeing the upside in events _____

SOCIAL AWARENESS

10. Empathy: Sensing other's emotions, understanding their perspective, taking an active interest in their concerns _____
11. Organizational Awareness: Reading the currents, decision networks and politics at the organizational level _____
12. Service: Recognizing and meeting follower, client or customer needs _____

RELATIONSHIP MANAGEMENT

13. Inspirational leadership: Guiding and motivating with a compelling vision _____
14. Influence: Wielding a range of tactics for persuasion _____
15. Developing others: Bolstering other's abilities through feedback and guidance _____
16. Change catalyst: Initiating, managing and leading in a new direction _____
17. Conflict management: Resolving disagreements _____
18. Teamwork and collaboration: Cooperation and team building _____

Based on the work of Daniel Goleman, Richard Boyatzis and Annie McKee,

Primal Leadership, Harvard University

YOUR 5 MOST IMPORTANT
LEADERSHIP COMPETENCIES

1. _____

2. _____

3. _____

4. _____

5. _____

YOUR 5 LEAST DEVELOPED
LEADERSHIP COMPETENCIES

1. _____

2. _____

3. _____

4. _____

5. _____

Take a look at the 18 competencies Daniel Goleman outlines in *Primal Leadership* to understand the competencies needed during each of the various 7 Stages of Growth. With this knowledge, leaders are better able to adapt, respond and hire accordingly.

LEADERSHIP COMPETENCIES
IN STAGE 1, 2, 3 AND 4

STAGE 1	STAGE 2	STAGE 3	STAGE 4
EMOTIONAL SELF-AWARENESS	EMOTIONAL SELF-AWARENESS	ACCURATE SELF-ASSESSMENT	ADAPTABILITY
SELF CONFIDENCE	ACCURATE SELF-ASSESSMENT	ACHIEVEMENT	ORGANIZATIONAL AWARENESS
EMPATHY	EMPATHY	DEVELOPING OTHERS	SERVICE
INSPIRATIONAL LEADERSHIP	INITIATIVE	CONFLICT MANAGEMENT	DEVELOPING OTHERS
DEVELOPING OTHERS	DEVELOPING OTHERS	TEAMWORK AND COLLABORATION	TEAMWORK AND COLLABORATION

Chapter 4:
The Challenge of Being
a Great Manager

I believe every single person who joins a company has the intention of becoming a valuable member of the team. The excitement level is high when employees start a new job. They're eager to learn, they want to excel and they believe they're making a good step in their own career path. They want to prove themselves. They want to belong. They want to be recognized. They want to like their co-workers and be liked. They want to know the boss knows who they are. They want to contribute. They want to be proud of the company they work for and they want their circle of family and friends to be proud of them for landing a new job.

Then, something happens that shakes their confidence. In many cases, that "something" is an inexperienced or simply bad manager. Your responsibility, as the CEO, is to ensure that your managers are skilled in growing and developing people. They need to be emotionally intelligent leaders. They must know how to set up systems that motivate people to deliver your products or services efficiently. They need to be proactive when it comes to managing the people issues in your organization because *people are your business.*

The Gallup Organization, probably the go-to-organization for statistics on employee engagement and managerial performance indicators, says, "If great managers seem scarce, it's because the talent required to be one is rare." Gallup's research reveals that about one in 10 people possess the talent to manage.

No wonder great managers are hard to find! In fact, also according to Gallup, "companies miss the mark on high managerial talent in 82% of their hiring decisions." And we wonder why we have a crisis of employee engagement in the U.S. and all over the world?

Toxic managers run rampant the world over, regardless of the company's size. I've seen toxic managers in small organizations with only 25 employees, and toxic managers in Fortune 500 companies that were designated as one of the best places to work.

I absolutely believe managers who run roughshod over employees, who demean, disrespect, bully and harass should be fired immediately. Their behavior is easy to spot – but getting rid of them seems to defy reality.

As I was writing this book, an employee at one of the world's most valuable startups, committed suicide. In a conversation right before his death, he confided to a friend, "That this place has broken me to a point where I don't have the strength to look for another job." Three lawsuits were pending, filed by employees who said the culture was one of sexual harassment and verbal abuse from managers.

Where does the blame lie? Directly at the CEO's feet. To allow toxic managers to treat people unfairly should never be tolerated.

Whenever I read about mistreatment, or see it first hand, I know the fault lies with the CEO.

MORE MONEY AND A NEW TITLE DOES NOT MAKE A MANAGER

All too often, good sales people, exceptional project managers, specialized production people, are promoted because leaders want to reward people who are good at what they do. And putting them into a manager role is a promotion and along with that comes more money. What person would pass that up?

I've done just that. I took a great writer and promoted him to the Manager of Writing Services. New title. New salary. Bad choice. He was a WRITER, not a manager. He loved writing, not managing writers. I kept him there, believing he would become a good manager through experience and coaching. The new position was exciting in the short term, but eventually his inability to manage our writing processes, deal with our inside account managers and our clients, led to a writer staff revolt. They disliked his approach, didn't like his attitude and hated how he kept all the interesting writing work for himself, and only delegated tasks he didn't like to do.

Eventually I had to let him go. My fault. I lost a great writer, created a whole lot of frustration and stress on a good group of people and learned another lesson, again. Don't promote people into management positions until you find out if they have a talent for managing people and enjoy the challenge of managing people. A critical question that got lost in the "would you like to become a manager and earn a whole lot more money" approach was this simple question:

"Do you enjoy working with, developing and helping people?"

We learned the hard way that great experience, good attitude, great work ethic doesn't always equate to a great manager. It can and you need to ensure you have a management development program in place to evaluate if that great employee can become a great manager.

WHAT MAKES A GREAT MANAGER?

Two words. They care.

Too simple? Probably. But my own experience tells me that the best managers are people who really care about people. This is a skill and a talent that can't be faked, but it can be improved. No question that developing good coaching skills, becoming a better communicator, enhancing your ability to be a good listener, learning how to set expectations and manage to those expectations are all necessary skills one must master to become a great manager. However, the drive to become a better manager starts from within. It starts with your own awareness of what makes a great manager and how much your care.

I started my career in Parks and Recreation at the age of 24. I was responsible for several recreation centers and the leaders who ran those facilities. I was young and ambitious. My ability

> The drive to become a better manager starts from within.

to get work done was recognized early on as a valuable trait that has served me well throughout my life.

However, I wasn't a good manager. I had no training in the art of managing people so I made a lot of mistakes. I expected people to work as I did. I expected them to be as ambitious as I was. I expected people to stay late when needed and not complain, because that's what I did. When I told someone to do something and they didn't do it, I got angry and confronted them. They, in turn, got defensive. I assumed they didn't care as much as I did.

In other words, I made managing people *all about me*, not about them. And they resented me because of my approach and pushed back even harder. I was miserable and knew the people who worked for me were miserable also.

Fortunately, I recognized my failings and signed up to get a Master's Degree in Public Administration. When I read the curriculum for the two-year accelerated program, I zeroed in on the topics related to "Managing a Workforce," and "Why People Skills Matter."

That program taught me about the art and science of management. I learned that a manager's sole purpose was to develop and help people grow. I learned that people are individuals and as a manager, you have to understand first who people are, and explore their goals and dreams to help them be the best they could be. I learned that managing wasn't about telling people what to do, but engaging them in the vision of the organization and helping them see how their role plays into achieving that vision. I learned the value of listening to what was being said instead of coming to a conversation with my own agenda.

I also learned about "situational leadership" developed by management expert, Ken Blanchard. You can't apply a one-size-fits-all approach to people. They want to be given direction, but they don't want to be micromanaged. Even back in the late 70s, we were taught to understand what each person's true talents were and to encourage them to bring those forward every day. I learned the importance of clear and consistent communication – of clarifying expectations and holding people accountable.

The degree offered hands-on learning. I dedicated myself to taking the concepts and exercises I learned in the program back to my job and practiced on my staff. I listened. I asked questions. I taught myself to be patient. I encouraged my staff to challenge me on things they didn't understand. I become a better manager.

Today, my approach is still anchored in the lessons I learned in those classes. My real advantage was that I simply cared about people. I hated that I wasn't being effective. I didn't want an angry bunch of employees. I wanted to help them be the best they could be. I just didn't have the skills.

You may be born with certain competencies such as empathy, optimism, initiative, service but most people aren't born to be great managers. You have to learn. You have to work on it. You gotta wanna!

As I developed skills as a manager, I moved up in my career and was able to impact people's lives as mentioned earlier. Your impact as a manager isn't obvious every day but an exceptional manager leaves a legacy. We need more exceptional managers to restore people's confidence in big business and to ignite the economic engine of this country through small business.

When I was working with Fischer, we helped one of our clients construct a Management Charter. I share it with you because of the value I saw it have on the each and every employee. The words meant something because they had a hand in sculpting the words.

MANAGEMENT CHARTER

- We believe that Our Company is a living intelligent entity, which exists separate from any owner, executive or staff member and that all members of the Company community work for and with this living business entity.

- We believe that People are the most important focus in this business. Without the full presence of each person in the enterprise the overall quality of the company is affected. Management is empowered to:

  □ Respect the dignity of the individual

  □ Acknowledge performance and participation

  □ Facilitate workplace satisfaction

- We believe that decision making, when shared by management with all employees, can explode the voltage of individuals within the company to take responsibility for the health and vitality of the enterprise. Management is empowered to:
  □ Encourage innovative thinking

  □ Share in the decision-making process

  □ Do the right thing

- We believe that when leadership skills are developed within every employee, the company experiences an explosion of growth and expansion. Management is empowered to:
  - Ask people to lead and expect them to be accountable
  - Set the direction and pursue the outcome
  - Dissolve the boundaries – demonstrate "we are they"

- We believe that active communication occurs in a company culture that encourages truthful communication. The unattractive alternative creates blocked communication resulting in the heavy costs associated with mistakes due to not enough or incorrect information flows. Management is empowered to:
  - Tell it like it is
  - Listen to understand
  - Utilize positive interaction

- We believe that trust is a critical building block for both management and staff to perform at their highest. Management is empowered to:
  - Delegate responsibility
  - Transfer authority
  - Leave the past behind

- We believe that agreements are the basis for integrity in the organization. Management is empowered to:
  - Confirm understanding
  - Do what you say you will do
  - Renegotiate when conditions change

- We believe that innovation is our competitive edge in the market place. Management is empowered to:
  - Ask for solutions
  - Allow freedom to make mistakes
  - Let no idea be too small

- We agree to support, manifest and advance the mission, values and objectives of The Company.

This was signed by all employees and hung with pride on the wall so employees and customers alike could see it as they entered the lobby.

EXCEPTIONAL MANAGEMENT ACCOUNTABILITY TOOL

In 1999, the year it was first published, I read Marcus Buckingham and Curt Coffman's book, *First Break All the Rules*. Both Buckingham and Coffman worked for Gallup, which for more than sixty years has been a world leader in the measurement and analysis of human attitudes, opinions and behavior. The book was the first to present an essential proven measuring stick linking employee opinions to productivity, profit, customer satisfaction and turnover rate.

The book uncovered a total of 12 questions in an in-depth study of over one million employees and eighty thousand managers. These 12 questions are based on research conducted by Gallup to improve engagement and ultimately, your bottom line. To learn more about the 12 Questions, buy the book today and embrace its insights. Stop making this harder than it needs to be.

As a manager, I used the 12 questions monthly with my management team. Each month, my managers were required to ask a specific question or two from those 12 questions, capture the responses from each direct report and share those results with me. I would then work with that manager and that employee to make sure we were addressing any specific concerns.

At the time, our company was in Stage 5 (58 – 95 employees): we had 84 employees, our revenues had increased by 41% and our staff by 21%. Our revenue per employee showed we were not hiring ahead of our capacity. We finished 1999 with the strongest net profit in 12 years of being in business. As with most other small businesses, we struggled with performance management indicators, holding people accountable and tracking performance to salaries.

Utilizing the concepts from *First Break All the Rules* helped us focus on research proven critical issues that employee's cared about. It made sense to incorporate those 12 questions into our management development program.

7 EFFECTIVE MANAGEMENT PRACTICES TO BUILD BETTER MANAGERS

Over the years, I've met many smart people who are in the same business I am – helping CEOs build great companies. A good friend and very smart business advisor gave me his 7 ways a manager can become more effective and valuable to those they supervise and those they report to. Ken Keller runs Strategic Advisory Boards out of his office in Valencia, CA and his straightforward, no-holds-barred communication strategies resonate with CEOs everywhere.

1. **Work with every direct report.** Don't ignore anyone. Spend more time coaching your best people simply because they can benefit from that kind of guidance. Spend time counseling the rest on how they can improve. Put action plans into place for each and hold them accountable for meeting deadlines.

2. **Learn each direct report's strengths.** When people use their strengths, they feel more competent and that they're making a contribution. Engaged employees require fewer management resources.

3. **Don't duck discipline.** Managers have a responsibility to enforce company policy. That means you must discipline people who violate standards, policies and procedures. When someone operates outside of what has been established, the manager needs to call the employee on that specific issue as soon as possible.

4. **Overcommunicate.** Every company has a disease, and the symptoms often surface through whining, complaining, denial and indignation. The disease is NETMA, which means No One Ever Tells Me Anything. Every important message, deadline and event must be repeated, over and over again, just in case someone has the disease on any given day.

5. **Know your limits.** Too often, people are promoted to a position to manage others because they are technically the best. Horror stories abound of the top-selling sales person who becomes the worst possible sales manager, or the best engineer who gets promoted to manager and fails miserably. Technical skills are very different from management skills. Managing is all about getting work done through the efforts of others instead of personally doing it.

6. **You're the bridge.** Management is the bridge between a company's top leadership and those doing the actual tasks required for the company to serve its clients. A manager must understand the larger picture of what's happening on a strategic level, and be able to translate that into tactical action steps down the line. The manager, more than anyone else, needs to be clear when communicating, keeping in mind that every employee has a WIIFM mindset: What's In It for Me?

7. **Routinely reappraise**. Regularly meet with each employee and ask six important questions. The answers are a mini-performance appraisal for manager and employee.

   □ Do you know what's expected of you at work?

   □ Do you have the materials and equipment you need to do your work right?

   □ Do you have the chance to do what you do best every day at work?

   □ In the past week, have you received recognition or praise for doing good work?

   □ Do I, as your manager, or does someone else here at work, seem to care about you as a person?

   □ Is there someone at work who encourages your development?

According to Ken, "The next few years will be brutal for small and midsize businesses. It will be an employee's market. If you want to keep your best employees, now is the time to strengthen your management skills, and those of every manager at your company. Otherwise, don't be surprised when your best people get poached."

Remember, while management talent is hard to find, you can develop, nurture and teach management skills to a willing learner. Can you identify someone in your organization today who already has the seeds planted to become a great manager? Look around. What do you see in terms of their strengths? Spend time with this person. Ask questions. What do they see for their future?

Helping people see beyond their own limited perspective is what being a great manager is all about. Managing people isn't easy. That's because people aren't perfect, so working with them isn't going to be perfect either. However, ignoring your role as a manager by not setting clear expectations is a cop-out. All too often, we assume people just know what they should do, or we assume they know what we want them to do. Our employees are not mind readers; they need to be told what you expect, in detail. By setting and managing expectations, you'll get better results, you'll create better rapport with your staff and you'll increase staff buy-in.

In a survey conducted by Opinion Research Corporation, American workers were asked to select the one trait that was most important for a person in a leadership role – that trait was "leading by example." More than anything else, employees want leaders whose beliefs and actions line up. Great managers walk quietly and leave lasting footprints on the minds of everyone they touch.

> Great managers walk quietly and leave lasting footprints on the minds of everyone they touch.

CASE STUDY: LETTING GO TO LET IT GROW?

Stage 3, with 20 – 34 employees, is the toughest transition for a business owner to make. It's the first time the company moves from CEO-centric to Enterprise-centric, meaning the CEO can no longer manage all the moving parts of the business. He must start "letting go to let it grow." CEOs often hit Stage 3 and ignore the warning signs, which leads to building frustration and burnout. Many CEOs try to simply keep doing what has always worked in the past.

Not Dan Benamoz, founder and president of Pharmacy Development ment Services (PDS) in West Palm Beach, Florida. Dan embraced the 7 Stages of Growth model and helped the company he had run for 18 years transition from being a successful entrepreneurial company to a successful managed company. PDS now has new leadership, an aligned and engaged management team and a clearer understanding of what they need to do to stay ahead of their growth curve.

Dan started his career as an independent pharmacy owner. He discovered that pharmacy schools across the nation let young graduates into the world with a shiny degree, but woefully inadequate business skills.

PDS launched in 1998 with the goal of providing independent pharmacy owners solid business, leadership, and financial knowledge necessary to run a thriving business in today's rapidly changing environment.

Pharmacy ownership can be an unfair game due to the Pharmacy Benefit Manager's (PBMs) inequities and decreased margins to Direct and Indirect Renumeration. When PDS reached out to pharmacy owners, the goal was to help them become and remain profitable.

PDS teaches pharmacy owners:

- Innovative programs, products and services the competition doesn't offer, but the community needs.
- How to be a more dynamic leader of a high-performing team with a great culture and not just another script counter.
- Proven strategies to help your team carry ideas across the finish line.
- Access to like-minded individuals, who traveled the same paths and were willing to connect and share their best practices.

Many years and hundreds of highly-successful pharmacies later, PDS's team of Business Coaches, Performance Specialists, Subject Matter Experts and Quality Assurance Analysts are working toward a common goal of helping as many independent pharmacy entrepreneurs as possible reap the financial and personal rewards of successful pharmacy ownership.

I started working with Kelley Babcock, PDS's Chief Operating Officer in November 2015. She was looking for support and guidance to better understand the challenges PDS was experiencing as it grew. As the COO, Kelley knew growth was taking a toll on her, her employees and the CEO. She knew I had been a COO who had taken a company from 2 to over 100 employees, and she wanted my insight and advice on how to better manage the changes associated with growth. In our first conversation, Kelley outlined some of the challenges she struggled with:

- Evaluating the organization's structure
- How to better understand the role she should play and the role, Dan, the CEO should play
- Defining strategy vs. goals – she and the CEO didn't agree on these
- Improving sales
- Making sure the right people were in the right seats

During our first conversation, I introduced her to the 7 Stages of Growth. I learned they were a Stage 3 company with 34 employees, on the cusp of becoming a Stage 4 company with 35 – 57 employees.

The business was solid financially but it seemed everything was a fire drill. She felt that Dan, the CEO, was still too involved in the day-to-day operations, which created confusion between what Kelley was doing and what Dan did. This caused friction between them, which made it harder for them to communicate effectively.

There was a lack of emphasis on sales goals and key indicators that could be tracked and measured, which bothered Dan. Kelley found herself defending her current sales and marketing selections causing further friction between two people who, up until six months earlier, were in lockstep.

PDS was struggling with all of the Stage 3 challenges. I shared more of the Stage of Growth model with Kelley and Dan as we prepared for a Stages of Growth X-Ray™, a two-day workshop with the CEO and management team, in September 2016. I wanted them to understand their situation was typical, based on the research, and show them how to get ahead of their growth curve. They needed to:

- Focus on the right things at the right time
- Adapt the leadership skills to the needs of the company
- Predict how growth was impacting the company today

Prior to an X-Ray, I met with the CEO to share the results from online assessments the participants completed in advance and to explain what the process for the two-day workshop would look like. Dan and I got together for lunch the day before the X-Ray and I immediately sensed his frustration. He was a bit lost as to why things suddenly felt so out of control. He wasn't confident in the management team, and even though he greatly respected Kelley, he wasn't sure she had the skills to take them to the next level. The next words out of his mouth gave me hope that PDS would make it beyond Stage 3. He said, "I don't think I can either."

Dan explained the pharmaceutical world to me. I heard the passion in his voice he felt for the independent pharmacy owner. Since he started PDS in 1998, his vision has been to "transform pharmacy business owners into bona fide entrepreneurs and their dreams of success into reality." His admission that he was a "pharmacy guy," not a "business guy" was very typical of an entrepreneur who had a dream, developed the dream into a growing business and then found that the day-to-day challenges of dealing with people and problems was overwhelming.

As discussed in the previous chapter, one aspect of the 7 Stages of Growth is a hidden agent called The Three Faces of a Leader. Every day, a leader must bring a Visionary, Manager and Specialist face to the table to provide direction for the company. In Stage 3, the Manager Face is 60% and in Stage 4, it grows to 70%.

The message is that the CEO must recognize the importance of being a great manager and embrace all the competencies that support being great manager. This was one aspect of the model Dan focused on. Just that one hidden agent reinforced Dan's need to evaluate his own skills and decide if he was the right person to take PDS to Stage 4 and beyond.

I held the two-day X-Ray workshop with Dan, Kelley and 8 other team members. Two were brand new. Kelley had let the sales and marketing people go the week before. In Dan's opening words, his frustration was evident when he said, "I feel like a startup, 18 times." (PDS had been in business 18 years). He was tired and uncertain as to the outcome of our workshop. I knew I needed to engage this team, identify the critical issues facing the company and get the team aligned behind the work that needed to be done.

Our first discussion centered the company's top five challenges. This is a 50,000-foot view of critical issues and the team came up with:

1. The need to have better staff buy in
2. Employee turnover
3. Organization needs to understand how the company will grow in the future
4. Project management and resource coordination challenges
5. Staff morale and voltage challenges

Throughout the two-day process, we dove deeper into the issues that brought these challenges to the top of each person's priorities.

We then looked at their Builder/Protector assessment and found the ratio closer to a Stage 4 company (3 Builders to 2 Protectors) versus a Stage 3 company (1 Builder to 1 Protector). The purpose of this exercise is to find out where there is uncertainty, which leads to caution instead of confidence.

The assessment revealed "Leaders appear confused by shifting business goals and issues that are not well defined." And "Leaders lose sight of the larger picture by focusing too much on the day-to-day operational details of the business." The participants also agreed with the statement, "Business decisions are seldom, if ever, arrived at through a comprehensive analysis of problems, facts and working assumptions."

We discussed each of the 36 statements presented in the X-Ray assessment and what they meant for the company. Through the conversation, critical perspectives were uncovered. The dialogue become richer with suggestions about what initiatives could be put in place to help resolve their concerns.

The Non-Negotiable Rules (NNRs) assessments within the X-Ray process are where the rubber meets the road. If the 27 Challenges are a 50,000-foot view of the company, and the Builder/Protector assessment takes us down to a 20,000-foot view, the NNRs have us looking at the water's edge at sea level. This exercise uncovers the root cause of the challenges.

Because PDS was a Stage 3 company, and one of the rules of the 7 Stages of Growth is "What doesn't get done in any stage of growth, doesn't go away," they also addressed the NNRs for a Stage 1 and a Stage 2 company. The obstacles from previous stages of growth were creating a drag on the organization.

As the two-day workshop progressed, I noticed an increasing level of engagement from Dan. In the beginning, he was a bit withdrawn, he expressed his disappointment in the progress the company had made up to now, and was visibly upset with some of the outcomes from the assessments. As people opened up and we were able to actually put words to the problems PDS was struggling with, the energy in the room changed from hesitant to highly charged. Because the process allowed everyone to be heard, and because the focus was on the company, not a single individual, people stepped into the challenge of creating a dialogue around how the team would address the issues.

The take-away value from each participant is critical to the success of any X-Ray process. After two days, the Dan and his managers were able to create five top initiatives that everyone agreed to focus on. The purpose of each initiative was clearly stated, people stepped up and owned each of the initiatives and agreed on what the outcome needed to be.

With PDS, a common theme was uncovered – there was a widespread lack of communication. It wasn't only felt from the top down; it impacted PDS's ability to serve their customers and address critical issues quickly and effectively. Other revelations from the X-Ray process included:

- No telling what we can accomplish if we all pull in the same direction at the same time.
- Understanding the unfinished business that was holding us back from previous stages of growth.
- We are committed to excellence but we have to revise the map to achieve it.
- Impact of dashboards and key indicators to create accountability.

When I met with Dan and Kelley at the end of our second-day, Dan was thoughtful. He was much more confident in the team's ability to address the critical issues. He was also much clearer on what his role would be going forward. Another outcome that surprised the three of us was Kelley's clarity on the fact that she wasn't in the right role. Dan knew he wasn't the manager the company needed to move forward and Kelley was clear that she wasn't the operations person the company needed.

This quote from Dan illustrates the value of helping a team get clarity on critical issues.

> *"As a result of the Stages of Growth X-Ray™, our leadership team is more aligned than ever, with greater clarity and a shared purpose that will propel us toward our business goals and objectives. The leadership team is acting cohesively as a unit and working more collaboratively toward outcomes that will shape our organization in the years ahead."*
>
> - Dan Benamoz, President,
> Pharmacy Development Services

The changes needed for PDS to successfully navigate a new stage of growth were no longer vague concepts. A newly defined PDS was introduced at their Annual Conference in February 2017.

In a follow-up phone call 60 days after the X-Ray, I quizzed the team on the progress they had made on the five top initiatives. Everyone on the call made comments such as, "activity levels are increasing throughout the organization," and "confidence is increasing." Sales had gone through the roof, with 34 new members in Q4, surpassing the previous year's new member acquisition of 7 members in Q4.

As of Q2, 2017, they brought on 138 new members and met their retention goal of 81%. Kelley became Vice President of Member Performance, Jeff Philipp took on the role of CEO/COO (with rave reviews from the management team), and Dan is working with his Board of Directors, focused on new opportunities for PDS and new avenues of member acquisition. From Kelley and Dan's perspective: "Jeff's arrival at PDS was timely and has been a godsend...the exact leadership we needed to take us to the next level."

Of the five initiatives put in place during the X-Ray, two had been completed and progress on the other three had evolved with even more clarity of direction for the entire organization. Communications improved throughout the organization. Dan and Jeff meet weekly, the management team stayed focused on key indicators and the sales mindset that was discussed during the X-Ray is now part of everyone's performance goals.

By the end of June 2017, retention was up 18% over last year with a 158% increase in new enrollments. Their newest challenge? Keeping up with all the new members!

The lynchpin in PDS's success today was Dan's recognition that, while he was instrumental in growing and managing the company for 18 successful years, he wasn't the right leader to take it to the next level. Does PDS still need Dan's influence and vision? Absolutely. His vision to "transform pharmacy business owners into bona fide entrepreneurs and their dreams of success into reality," is alive and well thanks to a business owner who knew his strengths and wasn't afraid to admit his weaknesses.

Chapter 5:
Growth Trumps
Processes Every Time

As I've worked with business owners over the years, one thing has become clear: growth trumps processes every time. We add more employees but we don't set up recruiting, interviewing or employee development processes. We add more clients but we don't set up customer intelligence, customer service or customer reconnaissance processes. We build more products and add more services but we ignore project management systems, customer relationship processes or enterprise resource planning systems. We bring in more money, increase receivables, increase payables but we don't upgrade our financial systems.

When we think about entrepreneurs with the vision and the courage to start up a business, there is a perception that they rail against systems and a planned approach to growing a business. The assumption is that, by sheer force of

> By Stage 4, the need for systems and processes is at critical mass.

will, a laser-like focus on marketing or a lot of money, they build a framework for success without intentional processes or a detailed plan.

Magazines love to fan this misconception with headlines like "She started her multibillion dollar business from her mother's attic." The message is: "she got started without formal systems and processes, and she is successful." Budding entrepreneurs think they don't need those things either but nothing could be further from the truth. That billion-dollar business would never have evolved if systems and processes weren't driving every aspect of the company.

When a company moves through Stages 1 – 4, the focus is on evolving, testing, identifying, and practicing how to sustain a profitable company. By Stage 4, the need for systems and processes is at critical mass. Defining and establishing those systems and processes should be Priority #1 in Stage 4.

MASTER PROCESSES

While delivering a presentation to a group of business owners, I shared 14 Master Processes critical for a company to explore as they grow. These processes were uncovered as I was running our marketing/communications company. Only later, once I understood the 7 Stages of Growth, did I begin to think about which ones a company needed for each stage of growth.

I was explaining the value of thinking processes through for Marketing and Sales, when a hand shot up in the audience. It belonged to a woman who I knew to be a marketing consultant for large organizations. She took umbrage with me referring to "marketing process" and complained that by reducing marketing to a "process," I was making the act of marketing seem more difficult. Further, she said, "too many businesses already consider marketing an ancillary part of their business. By reducing it to a process, you are demeaning the activity." My experience has been just the opposite. By NOT thinking about the processes it takes to run a successful company, the activity itself is ignored.

When working with companies of all sizes, I identify which processes need to be added as a company grows through the different stages of growth. I call them "Master Processes" to elevate their importance of in the eyes of a business owner. As a Stage 4 company, the top gate of focus is Process. This is another reminder for a CEO to continually identify and keep focused on activities that help a company sustain profitability, performance and productivity.

Michael Gerber, author of the *E-Myth* and the *E-Myth Revisited*, refers to these processes as your franchise prototype. If you can clarify your processes and identify them by name, you can run your business instead of feel like it's running you.

Processes help everyone understand "how work gets done here." Employees are looking for clear direction from management. They want to know how work is done so they can feel good about the value they bring to the company. When people are forced to make it up as they go or they are reprimanded for doing something wrong when they were never taught how to do it right, morale suffers, quality suffers, client satisfaction suffers.

In his book, *Traction*, author Gino Wickman tells a story about a dog sitting on a nail. A gentleman walks up to a farmhouse. An old man is sitting in his rocking chair on the porch. His old dog is sitting next to him. The old dog is moaning, so the gentleman asks the old man what's wrong with the dog. "It's because he's sitting on a nail," the old man replies. "Why doesn't he move?" asks the gentleman. "Because it's not hurting enough for him to move."

This is a great example of what happens as companies grow. Business owners often become frustrated when they describe the chaos they feel in their business. They allow inefficient processes (or worse, no processes at all) to become the norm, and they only react when the pain from the nail becomes unbearable.

When asked about their quality control process, or their on-time delivery process, they mumble something about those processes having worked just fine before. The insinuation is that it's a people problem, not a process problem. I often hear these complaints: "No one pays attention." "No one is concerned about quality." "No one cares about getting things out on time."

When we dig deeper, the process is either non-existent, or as the company grew, no one was in charge of updating it so it's out of date, or no one uses it anyway.

Effective processes can be identified and implemented by following these four critical steps:

1. **Write it down.** To be effective, a process must be written down. This is a great opportunity to identify the participants who should be involved with this process. Who has the knowledge? Who uses this process every day? Who is impacted by this process? The people who actually use the process and are impacted must be a part of capturing and writing it down.

2. **Train.** Once it is written down, people need to be trained on how to work the process. Plan time for training otherwise it won't happen. Make it mandatory. Let your employees know you value training and want them to spend time getting trained.

3. **Follow the process.** Once they are trained, people need to follow the process. You must hold people accountable. How do you know it's being followed? If there is a breakdown in the process, stop and take time to debrief on what happened, why it happened and how to avoid it happening again.

4. **Review.** Each process needs to be reviewed every quarter or twice a year, to ensure that the process is still efficient and relative based on any changes that have occurred in the company. You have to make sure someone owns each process that has been implemented. They need to stay on top of any issues and collaborate with others to make sure changes are made quickly and efficiently.

By recognizing specific processes by name and defining the activities that occur under that process, a company is more likely to allocate resources to ensure these processes don't get ignored in the chaos of growth. Processes are both critical and cumulative. For example, if you took care of your Financial Master Process in Stage 1 with 1 – 10 employees, congratulations. If you're in Stage 4 and you're still struggling with the financial aspects of your company, it's time to focus on this Master Process before you get any bigger.

It's my intent to identify the 14 Master Processes and suggest a few activities that can become a part of them. Depending on your industry, you may call these by a different name, or identify different activities. Perfect. The goal is to get you thinking about what processes are important for you to focus on today. So, add your own, change the name, update or add to the list of activities.

THE 14 MASTER PROCESSES

1. **Financial:** the processes within a company that help forecast, strategize, capture, control and report on all financial aspects. These include:
   - Accounts Receivable
   - Accounts Payable
   - Profit Plan (budget)
   - Cash Flow
   - Profit/Loss Statement by Revenue Group
   - Balance Sheet
   - Revenue, Cost of Goods and Gross Profit by Revenue Group
   - Gross and Net Profit
   - Inventory Control

2. **Customer Intelligence:** the processes within a company that discover, uncover, address and realign the customer focus. These include:
   - Customer Reconnaissance
   - Customer Communications

- Customer Retention
- Customer Relationship Database
- Customer Complaint Resolution

3. **Sales:** the processes within a company that help turn a prospect into a customer, qualify a customer, shorten a sales cycle, create long term relationships and generate a flow of referrals and additional leads. These processes include:

   - New Customer Acquisition – Steps of the Sale
   - Well Defined and Proven Sales Process
   - Customer Touch Points
   - Customer Account Development – Recurring Revenue

4. **Marketing:** the processes within a company that help a company understand their target audience, position their products or services, solve customer problems and generate leads. These processes include:

   - Target Market Research
   - Target Customer Profile
   - Competitive Analysis
   - Go-to-Market Strategy
   - Lead Generation and Lead Tracking

5. **Production:** the processes within a company that explain how a product or service is designed, created and distributed. These processes include:
    - Design
    - Purchasing
    - Assembly
    - Line Production
    - Inventory
    - Quality Control
    - Shipping, Receiving, Delivery
    - Training

6. **Operations:** these processes include what is needed to keep an organization, a facility or a plant operational. These processes include:
    - Facility Management
    - Information Systems
    - Purchasing
    - Repair and Maintenance
    - Inventory
    - Safety
    - Emergency Management
    - Risk Management

7. **New Product/Service Development:** these processes are specific to researching, exploring, brainstorming and developing new products and services. These processes include:

- Marketing Reconnaissance
- Customer Reconnaissance
- Well-Defined Product/Service Plan
- Internal Evaluation of Skills
- Design and Testing

8. **Human Resources:** these processes are designed to manage the human side of an organization. These processes include:
   - Recruiting
   - On-Boarding
   - Salary Bands
   - Hiring and Firing
   - Employee Development
   - Employee Training
   - Management Training and Development
   - Conflict Management
   - Benefits

9. **Strategy and Planning:** these processes are designed to provide insight, project and position a company for the future and create a method to deliver, refine, rewire and create a profit on whatever product or service you offer. These processes include:
   - Stages of Growth X-Ray™
   - Short and Long-Term Planning
   - Hiring Plan for Future Skill Sets
   - Organizational Structure

- S.W.O.T.
- Profit Design
- Billable Hours Plan
- Efficiency Plan

10. **Forecasting, Tracking and Reporting:** these processes are designed to provide tools to meet the growing demand of a product or service, keep track of cost, volume and price and provide headlights for continual resource planning. These processes include:

  - Lead Generation, Tracking and Review
  - Sales Pipeline Development and Reporting
  - Cost of Goods Evaluation
  - Pricing Structure

11. **The Work Community:** these processes direct, encourage and promote the belief that people in an organization have control over their destiny in a way that promotes an atmosphere of engagement, caring, commitment and concern. These processes include:

  - One-on-One Employee/Supervisor Meetings
  - The Twelve Questions
  - Department Meetings
  - Company Meetings
  - Project Team Meetings
  - Unifying Employee Events
  - Company Health Survey
  - Conflict Resolution and Diversity Training

12. Project Management: these processes include the management of project plans that need to get accomplished in a set timeframe and within a set budget. These processes include:

- Selection of Team
- Technology Options
- Recording Processes and Procedures
- Budget Planning
- Scheduling/Time Frame
- Resource Allocation
- Monitoring Progress
- Risk Management
- Contingency Planning
- Evaluation of Results

13. Knowledge Management: these processes help organize the flow of important information, capture and protect the intellectual capital of an organization and improve the overall efficiency of an organization. These processes include:

- Identifying Critical Information
- Information Flow
- Patents
- Proprietary Knowledge
- Protection Process for Intellectual Capital
- Legal Documents
- Confidentiality and Non-Disclosure Agreements

14. Communications: these processes determine how a company communicates, what they communicate to whom and how and when communication happens. These processes include:
- Detailed Communications Plan
- Organizational Structure
- Internal & External Audiences

As with every aspect of the 7 Stages of Growth model, the goal is to help business owners "focus on the right things at the right time." You may not need all of these master processes today. Look at what stage of growth you are at today, and simply review how well you have implemented the current processes and any that show up in previous stages of growth.

Suggested cumulative processes by Stage of Growth™;

Stage 1 1 – 10 Employees	Stage 2 11 – 19 Employees	Stage 3 20 – 34 Employees	Stage 4 35 – 57 Employees	Stage 5 58 – 95 Employees	Stage 6 96 – 160 Employees	Stage 7 161 – 500 Employees
Financial	Sales	Production	Production	Financial	Financial	Sales
Customer Intelligence	Marketing	Human Resources	Operations	Sales	Production	Marketing
Sales	Operations	Forecasting, Tracking and Reporting	Project Management	Human Resources	Human Resources	Production
Marketing	Strategy and Planning	Project Management	Knowledge Management	Strategy and Planning	Forecasting, Tracking and Reporting	Human Resources
New Product/ Service Development	Work Community	Communications	Communications		Work Community	Work Community
Human Resources						Communications

118

As you look at the processes you have in place today, remember one of the rules of the 7 Stages of Growth indicates that "What you don't get done in any stage of growth, doesn't go away." The processes show up because of what's needed to stay ahead of your growth curve for that stage of growth. Use the check list below to stay on top of which processes you have completed.

☐ 1. Financials	☐ 6. Operations	☐ 11. The Work Community
☐ 2. Customer Intelligence	☐ 7. New Product/ Service Development	☐ 12. Project Management
☐ 3. Sales	☐ 8. Human Resources	☐ 13. Knowledge Management
☐ 4. Marketing	☐ 9. Strategy and Planning	☐ 14. Communications
☐ 5. Production	☐ 10. Forcasting, Tracking and Reporting	

In his book, *Traction*, Gino Wickman identifies the critical components a company needs to gain and sustain traction. This book is a must read for any organization that wants to tighten up their performance to increase profits. Not so big on the whole process challenge? Get help! The investment in outsourcing this work to a company or an individual who focuses solely on helping capture, implement, and train critical processes for small business will be repaid a hundred times over. More and more, CRM and ERP organizations have "resized" their product offerings to the small business environment. They recognize that a small company still needs software and hardware solutions without the big corporation price tag.

Challenge #1:
Project Management
and Resource
Coordination Challenges

L et's start with a definition of a project. A project is temporary in that it has a pre-determined start and end in time, scope and resources. A project is unique in that it isn't a routine operation, but a set of operations specifically designed to accomplish a singular goal. The development of software for an improved business process, building a bridge, the expansion of sales into a new market, the development of a new product or service – all are projects. And all projects must be expertly managed to deliver the on-time, on-budget results, and the learning and integration that organizations need.

Project management then, is the application of knowledge, skills, tools, and techniques to deliver the project successfully. It involves planning and the organization of a company's resources, which include personnel, finances, technology and intellectual property. The challenge of project management and resource coordination addresses the need for companies to recognize the importance of developing project management templates to make planning efficient and easily repeatable.

While resource allocation is an integral part of the project management process – i.e. what resources do you need for those projects – it also begs the larger question: how well are we managing resources throughout the company on a regular basis?

This is the #1 challenge for Stage 4 companies for three reasons:

1. The company is experiencing more complexity: more people, more systems, more clients, more revenue and more expenses. There is a requirement to recognize project management as a strategic tool to improve efficiencies.

2. The CEO has hired and trained managers to run specific aspects of the company. Those managers need to bring project management experience and skills to the company.

3. The need to manage resources effectively has never been greater.

Projects can be simple, such as putting in a new phone system, or complex, such as developing and implementing a new market strategy for expansion. All companies manage projects; therefore, all companies need to develop skills in project planning and resource allocation.

The project management challenge is all about figuring out how to standardize critical processes to improve workflow and increase the company's ability to sustain profitability.

Most companies are fairly good at creating kick off meetings where the project team is pulled together to discuss all aspects of the project. Responsibilities are fine-tuned, expectations are set, communication plans are put in place and timelines are identified. Weekly (or sometimes daily) project update meetings are scheduled with the intent of making sure everyone understands what's working, where issues are cropping up and who will handle those concerns.

What doesn't always occur are post-project meetings that allow the project team to actually evaluate and review what went well and where improvements need to be made. A company's goal is to identify what "good" looks like. What makes a project successful? In no particular order, these are the questions that must be answered after each project:

1. Did we meet our overall objectives?
2. Was the client happy?
3. Did we meet our budget projections? Were we over or under and if so, why?
4. Did we meet our timelines? Were we over or under and if so, why?
5. How well did our team perform?
6. How well did we manage our resources?
7. What could we have done better?
8. What did we do well?

This isn't a meeting where fingers are pointed and complaints are logged. It is a critical assessment of how well the project team performed. Without this serious and consistent review process, new projects will be underfunded, resources won't be allocated properly, timelines will be unrealistic and the bottom line will take a hit.

Taking project management and resource allocation seriously is a critical step in improving performance, productivity and profitability for a company with 35 – 57 employees.

EXERCISE #1: IDENTIFY SKILLS AND TALENTS FOR A PROJECT MANAGER

Every project needs a leader. So, the first decision that has to be made related to a specific project is who will be the project manager.

A project manager is the person who organizes and coordinates a project as a whole and who oversees the development of the smaller tasks that a project is broken down into. A project manager has to have the ability to see a project from two different viewpoints: as one large project with a start and end date and as a series of small tasks that also have their own start and end dates.

A project manager also must plan and ensure that the right resources are assigned to all aspects of the project, including people, equipment, supplies and vendors. He/she needs to be knowledgeable on every aspect of the project. They need to know the client, the requirements and the scope of the work as outlined in the project contract or agreement. They need to know everything, down to the smallest detail, that is needed to make a project successful. Their value is in the planning and the managing of the work, not getting involved in the actual doing of the work.

No matter the size or scope of a project, the required skills of a good project manager don't change. Here are the 7 key skills that an effective project manager needs to have.

1. Be a Leader and a Manager

Leaders share and communicate a common vision; they gain agreement and establish the direction and desired outcomes of a successful project. They are effective at motivating others. A leader recognizes the need to create and foster successful teams that know how to communicate with each other, respect the roles and responsibilities of other team members and acknowledge that the team, not an individual, is at the core of a successful project. Managers are results driven and focus on getting work done against agreed upon requirements.

A good project manager will constantly switch from a leader to a manager as the situation requires. Ignoring leadership and management skills for the sake of someone who is good at details, putting together quotes or bids, using project management software or any of the other skills that follow, is short-term thinking and creates more problems as the project develops.

People need and want leadership. They want to know that the person in charge of the project cares about their contribution and cares about the value they bring to the project. First and foremost, a good project manager understands that people, not systems, make projects successful.

2. Be an Excellent Communicator

If a person struggles with communicating, listening to others or dealing with conflict, they will fail as a project manager. A good project manager must be able to deal with a variety of personalities, oftentimes in very stressful situations. They must be able to communicate verbally as well as in writing. Project management depends upon everyone, at all phases of any project, large or small, understanding what is expected of them and what needs to happen throughout the project.

At the start of any project, a project manager should outline who will be responsible for what, what information needs to be shared with whom, and when. The project manager should determine how often certain information should be updated, evaluated and adjusted based on how the project is progressing. They should also decide how information will be distributed and shared: through texts, emails, certified letters, or addendums to contracts. Creating a communication plan is one of the first responsibilities of a good project manager.

3.   Set up and Manage Budgets

The ultimate responsibility of the budget for any project lies with the project manager. Even with a team of accountants, it's still the project manager's responsibility to prepare, write and monitor the budget. A project manager doesn't need to understand

accounting principles but they have to understand that
the budget is tied directly to the schedule of the project.
If the project manager isn't on top of the expenditures;
the wheels could come off the project very quickly.
Understanding the budget and the project scope
requires an individual who is able to focus on critical
details and keep an eye on the big picture.

4. Be a Problem Solver

This skill requires someone who can quickly assess a
situation, analyze the implications, look for alternatives
and communicate the changes or solutions effectively.
A good project manager actually anticipates problems
in order to be prepared. They think about legal issues,
payment concerns, supplier issues, safety matters and
personnel challenges. They are ready with "Plan B" at
all times and examine the impacts to the project that
aren't always evident on the surface. A good project
manager knows that it's not about IF a problem occurs;
it's about WHEN. And they pride themselves on being
ready for anything.

5. Be a Consistent and Competent Planner

A good project manager can think through all aspects
of creating a plan – from the project plan, to the risk
management plan, to the safety plan, to the emergency
plan, to the budget plan, to the personnel plan. A plan is
made up of multiple components and requires someone
who understands the details, the timelines, the financial

impacts and contingency planning. Plans are fluid. They provide direction but they aren't carved in stone. A project manager must be able to recognize the value of planning and embrace the fact that plans change, sometimes daily, and be able to respond to those changes with patience and calm to maintain a sense of confidence in the overall project.

6. Willingness to Learn

While the entire project depends upon the strong skills of a good project manager, they can't know everything. A good project manager recognizes their strengths and remains open-minded in order to improve their own knowledge base. If a project manager is unfamiliar with some aspect of the project, they need to be willing to admit as much, listen and learn. They don't have to become the expert, but they do need to understand how that piece of knowledge fits into the overall project. A project manager who believes they know everything, and gives the impression they aren't open to listening and learning will have personnel issues throughout the project. Being able to admit what they don't know and being willing to listen and learn is the sign of a self-aware project manager.

7. Be a Negotiator and an Influencer

Negotiating requires working with other people with the intention of coming to a joint agreement. Throughout the life of any project, there are constant opportunities to negotiate. A good project manager looks for opportunities to create a win-win with each negotiation. The art of influence is convincing the other person that your way is better – even if it's not what they want. The need to negotiate and the need to influence occur on all projects so being aware of the difference, and when to use which one, is critical to the success of the project.

THE VALUE OF IDENTIFYING SKILLS AND TALENTS FOR A PROJECT MANAGER

If you have taken the time and energy to establish a solid recruiting, hiring, on-boarding, training and development program for new hires, adding good project managers will not be that difficult. When you are intentional about who you hire, clear about the outcomes you want that person to achieve and supportive in helping them learn and grow, everyone wins.

As a marketing communications company, managing 180+ projects every day, we didn't immediately recognize the need to hire people with good project management skills. Our core competency was marketing and we focused our candidate search on finding great marketing talent. We had an important "ah ha" moment that sounded something like this: Should we be looking for project managers that can help our marketing strategists manage projects? That simple adjustment to the recognition that we were a project driven company, that delivered great marketing strategy, fundamentally changed who we hired and how the company was organized.

EXERCISE #2: WHAT MAKES A GOOD PROJECT PLAN

When it comes to project management, planning is one of the most important tasks a project manager undertakes. So many aspects of the project are dependent upon the overall plan and that success lies in the project manager's ability to put forward realistic time and resource estimates. So, the first thing a project manager should do is create the project plan.

Many project plans start with what is known as the "triple constraint." This is the quality or scope of the project, the costs associated (the required resources) and the time or the schedule of the project. To create a project plan, the project manager must know those three things and build the plan around each of them.

Scope: This is a clear, specific statement as to what has been agreed to be performed/achieved in a particular project. The scope lays out the functions, features, data, content, etc. that will be included in the project. The scope also clearly expresses the desired final result of a project.

Cost/Resources: Resources always cost money so these two concepts are interchangeable. When thinking about a project, you have to think in terms of manpower/labor, materials, and resources for risk management or any third-party resources that need to be secured.

Time/Schedule: Time in any project is analyzed down to the smallest detail. This includes the amount of time required to complete each and every component of the project. This is then further broken down into the time it takes for each task. From this analysis, it is possible to estimate the duration of a project and how many resources are needed.

Each project has priorities that help determine where the emphasis might land when thinking through the constraints. Is TIME the defining factor of the project? If a new building isn't built before a specific date, will the company lose contracts for work? Is SCOPE the defining factor? Will penalties be applied if the deadline date is missed? Is COST the defining factor? A grant is providing the funding for the project and that is the driver of how much can be spent.

Project planning is more art than science. Even with all the new and updated software planning tools, there are still too many mitigating circumstances that impact projects that software can't predict or address. However, doing the due diligence to utilize project planning software is a wise choice. Just plan time for your project manager to learn how to use the new software so it becomes a valuable tool instead of an interruption to their daily planning.

THE VALUE OF CREATING A GOOD PROJECT PLAN

An experienced project manager will be all over creating an effective plan. When you have a plan, you have something you can review. When you are intentional about tracking critical information, you can identify areas where you made or lost money. The triple constraints warrant serious discussion and raise issues about risk management, alternate plans when something goes wrong and financial focus to avoid losses. Without a plan, you can't effectively manage risk. Part of that plan must include the post-planning review meeting. Too often, companies move on to the next project without taking the time to examine the current project results. The excuse is always "we just don't have time."

As a Stage 4 leader working to turn over specific aspects of the company to qualified managers, focusing on project management planning isn't a nice to have. It's non-negotiable.

EXERCISE #3:
BEING INTENTIONAL ABOUT RESOURCE ALLOCATION AND KNOWING WHEN TO HIRE THE NEXT EMPLOYEE

The third part of this challenge is all about effective resource allocation. My own experience tells me this isn't something that gets a lot of attention in growing organizations. The challenge isn't so much hiring (more employees) or buying more stuff (computers, copiers, software, trucks, machines); it's knowing how to measure the performance of those resources to optimize their effectiveness.

When our workload increased, we hired more people. We didn't stop and think about how to better allocate resources to our projects. We were managing over 180 projects every day. Who had the time to stop and think about how we could be more efficient? We weren't talking about "overallocations or underallocations" as it related to how many hours our people were working. We were successful in spite of ourselves; a reality I think many small business owners understand.

My purpose in writing this book is to identify specific challenges a company with 35 – 57 employees experiences as they grow. And resource allocation is a huge challenge and not something that garners a lot of attention or discussion.

When I work with CEOs, the main question I hear is, "When should I hire the next employee?" Or, "When do we expand our plant facilities?" Or, "How do I know I can afford additional overhead?"

A key indicator we used at the marketing communications company I helped to run compared revenue to number of employees. From 1988 to 1989, we increased our staff by 140% but only increased our revenues by 67%. Our revenue per employee indicator was well below our goal of $100,000 per employee.

As we grew from 17 staff to 22 staff in 1993, our revenue per employee reached $109,900. Our staff level increased by 29% and our revenues increased 27%. A much better picture, but also an indicator that told us we weren't hiring faster than our revenues were growing.

Greg Crabtree, the CEO and founder of Crabtree, Rowe & Berger, an accounting firm in Alabama, believes the accounting industry has made finances too hard for business owners to really understand. In his book, *Simple Numbers, Straight Talk, Big Profits*, Crabtree does an incredible job of breaking numbers down in a way that anyone can understand. More importantly, he uses a system that focuses on "clearing the distortions" starting with owners who don't take salaries in order to enhance the net profits on the books. He also purports that paying taxes, instead of avoiding them, is the only way to grow a profitable business.

Crabtree believes that pretax profits should never be below 10% and that a business should plan toward 15%. If you are at 5% or below, your business is on life support and you will not survive. I fully enjoyed this advice, and now use it with my clients.

The premise behind Crabtree's "simple numbers" continues as he:

1. Breaks out labor costs and sets up a profit and loss sheet to identify direct labor, which he defines as people on your payroll who spend 50% or more of their time in revenue producing activities, without payroll expenses and benefits
2. Defines cost of goods sold as only costs that include materials, production supplies, subcontractors, direct travel (not direct labor – he separates direct labor from cost of goods)
3. Simplifies operating expenses into 5 categories: facilities, marketing, salaries for management and administration, payroll taxes and benefits and other operating expenses.

With this in mind, Crabtree believes every business owner should focus on the gross profit per labor dollar as the most important key indicator for labor productivity. If you can capitalize on controlling labor costs, profitability is much easier to maintain. Plus, you'll have a much better idea of how well your dollars are producing for every dollar you spend on labor.

Critical indicators include:

- Direct Labor Efficiency (DLE): Gross margin dollars divided by direct labor cost (not all COGS, just labor)
- Sales Labor Efficiency (SLE): Contribution margin dollars (gross margin minus direct labor) divided by sales labor cost
- Management Labor Efficiency (MLE): Contribution margin dollars (gross margin minus direct labor) divided by management labor cost

Crabtree addresses Stage 4 businesses in his book and refers to them as companies that generate $5 million and more in revenues. He maintains you must keep a 10% pretax profit (or more when you get this large) and leave any profits after taxes in the business to fund growth instead of relying on debt or outside capital. He believes you should constantly refine your management team. Evaluate their skills and knowledge in order to identify weaknesses in talent that could impact your ability to grow.

Crabtree employs an exercise based on the same concept that the NFL uses to determine their salary cap – how much they can spend on new talent.

Simplify your P&L and create what Crabtree refers to as your own "Salary Cap Exercise" by identifying:

- Revenues
- Pretax profits
- Non-salary costs, and
- Total expenses

Whatever is left over, you can use for salaries. Over your salary cap? You have some series decisions to make.

This chart is one of many from Crabtree's book and illustrates how to create your own Salary Cap. Brilliant! Get his book and take the mystery out of your numbers. Better yet, get real and get profitable.

SUMMARY OF SALARY CAP EXERCISE

REVENUE		$1,000,000
SALARIES	($450,000)	
NONSALARY COSTS	($400,000)	
TOTAL EXPENSES		($850,000)
PRETAX PROFIT (15%)		$150,000

At a 15% pretax profit, this company can spend $450,000 on salaries.

Knowing when to hire the next employee isn't a science; it's an art. There are many factors to consider. Fortunately, there is an easy-to-understand formula: labor efficiency. It's not a new concept but, thanks to Greg Crabtree, those of us who weren't born with a calculator for a brain can now utilize it.

In the early years of growing our company, we hired when we felt overwhelmed by the amount of work we were bringing in. When we landed a new client or a new project, we hired more people. Our formula was billable hours and we watched those carefully.

> Knowing when to hire the next employee isn't a science; it's an art.

We made sure all of our managers were at least 50% billable in order to maintain a specific net profit. There were very few staff members who we considered strictly overhead. When you hire more people, you must buy more equipment, you may need to expand your office space, and you pay more in benefits. As we grew and learned the value of profit planning, cash flow management, and capacity planning, we created a billable hour's formula that helped us know how much work we needed to land in order to maintain a level of profitability. That's what resource allocation is all about.

What does resource allocation look like for your company? Are you thinking about the number of employees you can afford based on how well utilized they are? Do you need to add more equipment? What/who do you need in terms of talent and skill to run that equipment? Do you have employees who aren't performing at their capacity? Are your sales goals keeping up with your growth strategy? Do you know what skills are needed for key positions?

THE VALUE OF BEING INTENTIONAL ABOUT RESOURCE ALLOCATION AND KNOWING WHEN TO HIRE THE NEXT EMPLOYEE

Growth hides many serious issues and those issues stay hidden underneath the surface of our organizations until something breaks. The break may be the loss of a huge account that you ramped up for by hiring more people or scaling up equipment. Or the break may be an outside force such as when the housing market collapsed in 2007.

Resource allocation isn't something you can ignore; in good times or bad. You have to create a plan. You have to understand the key indicators that spell success and let you know when things are working and more importantly, when they aren't working.

If you are a billable hours shop, you need to track every hour your employees work and be able to put a price tag on those billable hours to achieve a profitable end result. If you are a manufacturing shop, you have to understand efficiency ratios, how to manage waste, rework and inventory controls.

I encourage you to pick up Greg Crabtree's book and check out his YouTube videos. Getting focused on how you are spending and creating a plan will realign how you think about financials.

RESOLVING THE CHALLENGE OF PROJECT MANAGEMENT AND RESOURCE ALLOCATION

As a company grows, there are more people, projects, clients and more complexity; there must be more processes. The CEO can no longer be counted on to catch problems before they occur or to make all the decisions. As the company grows, overhead ramps up, and if someone isn't paying attention, profitability will begin to erode.

By Stage 4, the company has outgrown one person's ability to manage it all single handedly, and processes must become the leader's best friend as the company grows.

When the company has 20 employees, allocating resources to a project is easy. As companies grow, typically the leader continues to simply run the company without thinking intentionally about what resources are needed and why they are needed. Unless resources are effectively implemented, the business starts to break down.

What is your plan for this critical part of growing your company? If analyzing project management systems and resource allocation are not among your strengths, find the expertise to provide you with better insight. Take the time to understand the software options available for small to mid-sized business. The outlay of money will be more than offset by the efficiencies gained.

Staff morale and better bottom line results are great reasons to get focused on the processes and resources the company needs to succeed.

Challenge #2: Difficulty Diagnosing the Real Problems or Obstacles to Growth

The company I helped run was a marketing communications company. In our early years of growing the business, we primarily hired people with marketing talent and skills. We kept having issues. Those issues had everything to do with a lack of defined processes. People were tripping over each other due to the lack of defined roles and responsibilities. On the surface, it appeared to be a problem with people. Either we weren't providing the right training or they were the wrong people. Our fixes didn't solve the problem.

Here's why.

We weren't diagnosing the right problem. We were addressing surface issues, not the root cause of the problem. The real issue was we weren't hiring people with project management experience. We thought we needed to hire people with marketing experience. We assumed they would simply be able to figure out the project management side of the business. And we were wrong.

On any given day, we were managing 180 projects. We kept struggling to understand why our Account Managers and our Assistant Account Managers were having so much trouble staying on top of projects. We finally figured out that we needed people who were skilled in process management, at systems thinking; not just people good at marketing strategy. We defined marketing as our core competency, so we hired for marketing skills exclusively across the board.

Once we had our "ah ha" moment and figured out that we needed to hire people who were good project managers, things changed. Our Account Managers (our first line communicators to the client who needed to have very good marketing skills) got support from Project Managers who became the glue that kept all of the parts to each project functioning well.

The PMs were responsible for capturing the processes, following up with the Assistant Account Managers and making sure other key components of the company (our web designers, graphics staff, writers, technicians) got involved when they needed to be involved. This left our Account Managers free to focus on the clients' needs, instead of managing all aspects of the project. PMs changed our thinking and changed our ability to grow more effectively.

However, the biggest success was the PMs reduced the amount of stress and burnout our Account Managers experienced on a daily basis. Yes, it took time to re-think roles and responsibilities; it required a much more effective communication system to make sure everyone knew what was going on with each project. But the end results can be summed up in two words: Improved Moral!

When we stopped trying to pin our problems on people and people-related issues and took the time to look beneath the surface of the problem, people embraced the new processes. They felt as if they were able to focus on their strengths and what they loved doing. Our Account Managers took care of the clients and our Project Managers supported the projects. The other positive result over time was improved profitability.

When I conduct my Stages of Growth X-Ray™ program with CEOs and their management teams, the challenge of diagnosing problems is addressed. The program is designed to:

- Uncover the root cause of issues quickly (two days; not two months)
- Give everyone a chance to put words to their concerns (a series of online assessments help each person identify their issues by name)
- Create immediate buy-in from a facilitated session where we take the mystery out of running a company (too many assumptions that need to be addressed)
- End up with the top five initiatives that address immediate concerns, who owns those initiatives and the outcomes that can be expected when those initiatives are completed.

The reality is it's hard for executives to understand what their problems are. As the COO of that marketing communications company, I knew something wasn't right. I just couldn't put my finger on it so I guessed. I tried one solution and when that didn't work, I tried another. A lot of time, energy and money was wasted, not to mention the increasing frustration level and burnout felt by all employees. Sound familiar?

EXERCISE #1: CREATE AN ENVIRONMENT OF TRUST

This challenge is directly tied to a company's leadership. CEOs often assume they know what their problems are. If employees raise issues that don't align with the CEO's assumptions, those issues are often discounted. In this type of environment, employees simply won't speak up about problems. They don't want to be perceived as a whiner, a complainer, or someone who always sees the negative.

I refer to this dynamic as the CEO Disease. I used to suffer from it myself. I recall listening to an employee's concerns about how we did something and what wasn't working. What I heard was complaining. I remember thinking, "It's always worked in the past. What is this person's problem?"

Instead of really listening, I was already judging and assuming (two very, very bad traits in a leader) they were wrong, and what we had always done was right. Once I started to understand the dynamics of the 7 Stages of Growth, I became a better leader.

Ask questions to create dialogue. Business leaders should be open to hearing the good, the bad and the ugly. It should be the goal of every leader to uncover the truth behind any issue.

Many companies go the completely opposite direction and unwittingly create a culture of conflict. This can happen quickly when problems are looked upon as a result of someone not doing their job right. It goes back to the highly outdated (but sometimes still deeply ingrained) belief that employees are stupid and lazy.

Leaders who don't believe that people want to succeed and do a good job can't hide their underlying beliefs for long. They show up daily and erode morale. Plus, it's hard to talk to someone who gets defensive, reacts negatively to feedback and takes everything personally.

Ask questions to create dialogue.

CEOs need employees to feel comfortable to speak up, tell the truth about what's going on and raise their hand when there are issues. Creating an environment of trust is hard for some leaders but it can be done. Some suggestions on how to do so are:

1. Look and be approachable. When you walk into the office every day, engage in morning conversation with everyone you can. Make it a goal to talk to every single employee each week. With 35 – 57 employees, it's a reasonable mission.

    Smile. Engage. Ask questions. Talk about your weekend or your latest conversation with a client. Share some of your concerns. Find out about their weekend. What do they like most about their job? Make it a positive interaction. If you do this consistently, people will see you as a regular human being who just happens to run the company.

2. Create opportunities to meet with teams on a regular basis. If your managers have division meetings each week, attend and listen. Learn. Share your ideas. Don't solve. Ask questions. Be engaged. Show the team you respect and value the opinion and the work of their manager.

The value of this exercise is it shows your managers and their teams that you care about what's going on in their world; that you are relaxed and comfortable hanging out with them. It's easy for employees to put CEOs on pedestals or to fear them (it just comes with the title). It's your job to break down those barriers and show people you're interested in what they are contributing and the issues they are face.

3. Create social opportunities where the entire company can relax together. Make sure you are a part of that planning process. You don't have to manage it, but you have to be engaged and committed so people take these outings seriously. If you take them seriously, others will also. Make sure you are clear about the "why" of these events.

Don't be afraid to talk about the value of people getting to know each other outside of the work setting. Get employees involved in finding events people enjoy and mix them up. Some people will enjoy a BBQ with volleyball and others, who aren't sports inclined, might enjoy a more problem-solving activity such as an out of office scavenger hunt.

THE VALUE OF CREATING AN ENVIRONMENT OF TRUST

In order to create an environment where people will tell you what's happening in your company, you have to create relationships that are based on trust and encourage truth telling. When people feel safe to speak freely, they will work harder to find solutions and improve the way things are done.

In his book, *Why Employees Are Always a Bad Idea*, Chuck Blakeman points out that the Internet created what's known as the "Participation Age." A company's public face cannot be inconsistent with its internal face. The transparency of the Internet makes it harder for companies to talk out of both sides of their mouths. Plus, employees and customers can easily express their opinions online.

Blakeman maintains a company culture isn't something you sit down and create; it's a reflection of the CEO's behaviors and characteristics. If those behaviors are bad, the culture will also be bad. One of Blakeman's colleagues, Jason Fried, the co-founder of 37Signals (now Basecamp), supports this idea. He says, "You don't create a culture. Culture happens. It's the by-product of consistent behavior. If you reward trust, then trust will be built into your culture. Just do the right things for you, your customers and your team, and it'll happen."

You have to be able to create an environment of trust in order to consistently diagnose and ultimately solve the problems that create obstacles to growth.

EXERCISE #2:
CREATING A KEY
INDICATOR DASHBOARD

To more easily diagnose real problems, all Stage 4 companies need an instrument panel or dashboard that monitors pertinent and timely information. Using key indicators helps identify where the company is being successful, and more importantly, where problems might be surfacing. Sometimes these are called flash sheets or scorecards. It doesn't matter what you call it, it just matters that you track critical information: revenues, gross margins, net margins, sales pipeline, projects completed on budget, etc. in order to get to the bottom of your obstacles to growth.

However, keep it simple! Don't overcomplicate. Don't think you need 15 metrics when focusing on the top 3 will provide you with better results. Are you measuring the right things? If you select your employees' measurements, you are probably focusing on the wrong things. Get your employees to identify their own key indicators that tell them when things are going well or not. When a manager selects key indicators for team members, disengagement is not far behind. No one appreciates having numbers stuffed down their throats.

When every employee is involved in identifying their own key indicators, those issues become organizational challenges. The discussion to improve specific numbers is less personal. Key indicators take the emotion out of problems. They tell you the daily story of what is happening in the company. If you're not in touch with key metrics on a daily basis, you're flying blind, which forces the leader to go back to a trial and error mindset. Instead, this is the time to utilize the competency of an experienced management staff.

Open a dialogue around these key indicators. Ask questions and challenge assumptions. This is how good decision-making starts.

- What key indicators do we currently track?
- What additional key indicators should we track and report? Who needs to know about these key indicators?
- How should we provide this information to all employees?

THE VALUE OF CREATING A KEY INDICATOR DASHBOARD

If you measure it, you can improve it. We all know the value of this statement. Why, then, is it so hard for companies to 1.) determine what those key indicators should be 2.) identify how to measure the outcomes and 3.) hold people accountable to those key indicators?

The answer lies somewhere in the lament I often hear from managers: Why can't they just do what I tell them to do? In other words, the process for tracking key indicators from their perspective goes something like this: "I gave them their key indicators, I told them to track them, I asked that they report back to me on a regular basis and I get nothing!" The responsibility of setting key indicators doesn't lie with the manager; it lies with each employee. So, "giving them their key indicators" does not teach accountability.

My mantra regarding accountability and good management practices is simple: Set clear expectations and then follow up on those expectations. (The critical element here is follow up: great managers know the difference between follow-up and micromanaging.) Goal setting and key metrics go hand in hand. Help employees understand the relationship between these three critical steps and set up key indicators to track and measure:

Step 1: Company goals

Step 2: Department goals

Step 3: Individual goals

Each person in the company must understand what role they play in helping the company to reach its larger goals. The receptionist at the front desk should understand that his or her role is the first physical point of interaction with the external world and represents the organization as a whole. That individual must have key indicators that tell them how they are doing to help the company reach its big picture goals.

It really is that simple. And yes, it takes time. But what is more important than helping people be successful? I encourage managers to ask each direct report: What indicators, financial and non-financial, will tell you when you are being successful? I look for three to start with that are easy to track and measure.

As a COO, my "ah ha" moment came when I realized key indicators were not about the employees or me. They were about the company. If the company didn't succeed, we'd all be out looking for another job. I started thinking in terms of what was good for the company and those difficult conversations and the necessary follow up become a critical part of my daily world.

EXERCISE #3: CREATE AN ORGANIZATIONAL COMMUNICATION PLAN

According to Susan Scott, author of *Fierce Conversations*, people resent being talked *to*; we would rather be talked *with*. I agree. From my own experience, I know how devastating poor communication protocol can be to an organization. Making assumptions is the sign of an inexperienced or inattentive leader, and the repercussions can be extremely damaging.

Investigate the type of organizational communication going on in your company. Open lines of communication are imperative so that issues are reported throughout the organization productively. Employees must feel valued enough to supply honest feedback, and leaders need to be open-minded and receptive to feedback.

As a leadership team, discuss how your organization currently conducts:

1. Monthly company meetings

    a. Reports and key indicators from departments, divisions, teams; how well each group is doing to meet their goals, areas that need improvement and suggested solutions

    b. New clients: who are they and what you are doing for them?

    c. Financial status with relevant information as it pertains to teams, divisions, etc.

    d. New hires: who are they, what will they be doing and who do they report to?

e. Accolades: what or who has been successful and why (you can name individuals or teams)?

f. Q & A session: encourage participation

2. Team/Staff meetings

a. Reports from individuals and updates – things they are accountable for from the last meeting

b. Updates on key indicators and progress on projects

c. Critical issues: those that affect the entire group (individual issues should be discussed one-on-one with manager)

d. Accolades: what's working and why

3. One-on-one meetings with manager and each direct report

a. What did you do last week that you are proud of?

b. What would you like to learn next week to improve?

c. How can I help?

d. The dialogue is critical; after these areas are covered, encourage other conversations (to learn more about the One-on-One process, go to http://growasuccessfulbusiness.com/the-one-on-one-meeting and download this free report).

4. Anonymous organizational health surveys

a. Work with key employees and/or management team to either hire someone to provide this service or identify areas of concern and create questionnaires to address those issues.

b. Communicate the purpose of the survey in advance and let people know how the results will be handled.

c. Anonymity is important to allow people to feel comfortable sharing their thoughts even in a culture of open and honest communication; don't assume people are comfortable telling the truth.

d. Put a plan in place to share the results of the survey, create follow up conversations around the results, and create teams of employees to put solutions in place for the top issues.

e. Continue to talk about the results and the solutions in every monthly company meeting.

5. Unifying events for employees

a. What activities will engage people? One size does not fit all.

b. Create employee teams to promote and organize these events. Don't let this be an HR function.

c. Identify those events in advance and give people plenty of time to plan on attending.

d. The CEO should be the champion of these events and be present and engaged.

e. Talk about the events at monthly company meetings to either report on how well they were attended and/or remind people they are coming up.

These activities promote effective communication and should be a part of a company's planning process to promote an organizational culture. Always encourage employee interaction and feedback.

Every company should have its own Communications Plan. Here are some guidelines to consider:

#1: Determine what information needs to be communicated

    a. What are the top 5 challenges for your company's Stage of Growth?

    b. Who are your top 3 competitors and why?

    c. What is your vision, mission and values?

    d. What is your growth strategy?

    e. How will each employee impact that strategy?

    f. What are your daily key indicators by department and for the company?

#2: Determine how information will be communicated (email, formal memo, meetings, online newsletter)

    a. NEVER allow negative information to be sent via email

    b. Reduce email communication and increase face-to-face communication

    c. Outline and discuss your social media policy

#3: Design a program (such as one-on-one meetings between supervisors and direct reports) that encourages consistent and intentional communication with all employees

a. Managers should meet weekly with direct reports

b. Encourage dialogue around 3 key areas:
   feedback, employee development and employee
   performance

#4: Develop a protocol that encourages successful meetings for the company, teams, divisions and one-on-one

a. Weekly manager/employee meetings

b. Monthly company meetings

c. Weekly division/team meetings

#5: Determine what information needs to be transferred to other people in your company

a. Solutions to problems encountered

b. Success stories

c. Introduction of new employees

d. Immediate changes in critical key indicators

e. Project updates with milestones met and/or
   missed

#6: Determine how you will capture and transfer that information

a. Customer Relationship Management and/or
   Enterprise Resource Planning solutions

b. Notes from meetings posted on intranet

c. Online newsletter

d. Weekly email updates

#7: Determine what the CEO/Partners know that others need to know

    a. Status of sales compared to projections

    b. Status of expenditures compared to projections

    c. Gross margin updates on all revenue groups compared to projections

    d. Successful new client acquisitions

    e. Competitor updates

    f. New opportunities

#8: Determine what managers know that others need to know

    a. Project updates compared to projections

    b. Capacity planning, workload planning

    c. Division and department updates

#9: Determine what the staff knows that others need to know

    a. What is working and what isn't working?

    b. What contacts/clients are saying and responding to

    c. Success stories

    d. Solutions uncovered, problems solved

#10: Determine what individual teams know that others need to know

    a. What worked and what didn't work?

    b. Project milestones

  c. Success stories

  d. Customer's input

THE VALUE OF CREATING AN ORGANIZATIONAL COMMUNICATION PLAN

When we experience problems with our staff, there's usually an underlying communication malfunction.

This could mean:

- Something that should have been said, wasn't.
- Something that shouldn't have been said, was.
- Someone said something that wasn't true.
- Someone made something up because they didn't know the truth.
- Something wasn't communicated fast enough, to the right person.

Most issues start because of a lack of communication and most issues remain unresolved for the same reason. If you aren't intentional about communication activities, critical aspects of your operation aren't communicated to the right people at the right time. And more than likely, your communications don't occur as frequently or consistently as they should. Start being intentional about communication.

RESOLVING THE CHALLENGE OF DIFFICULTY DIAGNOSING THE REAL PROBLEMS OR OBSTACLES TO GROWTH

Rarely are CEOs able to see the entire picture. Employees are guarded in how they deal with their managers. They observe their manager's behaviors when issues or problems are brought to the table and assumptions are made all over the place.

If managers are experienced and confident in their roles, those issues are embraced and an open dialogue ensues. If managers view issues brought to their attention as a direct affront to how well they are managing, their demeanor can shut down a conversation. Employees will stop bringing issues to the table because they don't want to deal with their manager's anger or impatience.

A critical step in uncovering obstacles to growth is to offer a discovery process. This is an opportunity for employees and managers to flush out ideas and issues and people are given a language to identify the problems they face.

In delivering the Stages of Growth X-Ray™ program to CEOs and management teams, the most revealing outcome is the ability to put words to their pain.

For example, the following statements are included in the Stage 4 X-Ray questionnaire and tend to elicit strong responses from participants:

1.   There are defined roles and responsibilities for all department manager positions.

2. We identify key systems required to sustain enterprise health and improved performance.
3. We've identified our top 10 master processes.
4. We train all management staff on our project management template.

Each person responds on a scale of 0% (we don't do this at all) to 100% (we do this all the time). When I facilitate this process, I don't focus on the score. I focus on the conversation we're going to have when someone says: I have no idea what our top 10 master processes are. Then we start the dialogue that helps everyone understand what master processes are, which ones the company has in place today and which ones they need to put in place. The process helps us uncover the root cause of issues quickly (two days not two months) and gives everyone a chance to put words to their concerns.

> *"As a fast-growing company, we found ourselves struggling to keep our focus on the areas of our business that were critical for sustainable progress. In fact, we didn't really know what those areas were. We engaged Kate Ripp from Mission Critical Teams to facilitate the 'Stages of Growth' program with our leadership team and through this process we have discovered what our current operational environment truly is, identified the critical path items and objectives that will guide us to our next growth objective, and developed a strategic vision and set of key initiatives that will become our roadmap for ongoing progress.*
>
> *We feel we are working more cohesively as a team and setting our sights above the day-to-day distractions that take away from our ability to see and accomplish our future objectives."*
>
> -Jeff Bay, Managing Director
> *HayMax Hotels, Aspen, CO (Growth Curve Specialist, Kate Ripp)*

The ability to diagnose the real problems or obstacles inhibiting growth starts with leadership's philosophy about how to effectively communicate and deal with challenges. Without the ability to have real conversations that get to the heart of an issue promptly, a company can quickly become bogged down. Get ahead of your growth challenges and start a dialogue.

Challenge #3:
Employee Turnover

I'll introduce the challenge of employee turnover by asking a few questions that I believe are at the heart of the issue:

- Do you take the time to help your managers understand what you expect from them and what they can expect from you?
- Do you have a strong relationship with each of your managers?
- Do you know if your employees respect their manager?
- How well do your managers connect with their staff?
- Are managers getting the best out of each person?
- How do you track a manager's performance?
- Are managers working with direct reports to set clear expectations, establish key indicators and then managing to those expectations?
- Do you have a leadership development program in place? If the answer is yes, is it effective?

If the answers aren't a resounding **Yes** across the board, you probably have a high employee turnover rate, or you have underperformers who are slowly sucking the life out of your business.

Each of these questions should force you to intentionally think about the reasons great people stay with your company. If you aren't connected with each manager, how can you know how well that manager is connecting to his/her direct reports? The short answer is you can't. High employee turnover begins when a CEO is out of touch with her managers.

While the CEO has to continually keep the big picture in mind and plan for a company's expansion, she can't afford to take her eye off how well each manager is doing the job they were hired to do.

When we find great employees, it's our job as leaders and managers to keep them. The disturbing reality, according to a variety of different studies and Jeffrey Pfeffer's book, *Leadership BS*, "The vast majority of employees are unhappy with their work, disengaged and hoping for a different job. And more to the point, employees are unhappy with their leaders. Very, very unhappy."

The challenge of employee turnover has many underlying issues. To get on top of it, CEOs need to:

- Understand what positions are needed to move the company forward to ensure that they know what to look for when hiring people
- Know what skills and talents are needed today and for future growth, and map those skills to positions so the people you hire can perform the work needed
- Set clear expectations for all employees and then manage to those expectations, which requires

performance management systems that instill standards and measurements

The fact is, regardless of the systems you have in place, you will have employee turnover. How you manage it is the test of how well you "walk the talk" regarding the culture of your organization.

When our marketing communications company started to grow, it became more and more difficult for me to interview all the potential candidates for various positions. When new people were hired, I spent 30 minutes with each one. This time became known as "Laurie's Rant." My message was this: There are behaviors we want to see exhibited and those behaviors are guided by our values. There are behaviors we don't tolerate and these are the behaviors that can get you fired.

Experience showed that beating around the bush about what we needed to see from new people coming on board was a waste of my time. It didn't really help the new person understand what they needed to do to succeed either. My intent at this meeting was to explain our culture and explain how our values play out every day through examples. I wanted to let them know we cared about them as individuals and we were there to help them be successful.

I recall one time; I finished my rant about our values and our belief in our people with a new employee, Wayde. As he got up to leave my office, he said: "All that sounds great, Laurie. And here's my challenge to you. If, after 30 days, I see examples of what you are saying, I'll buy you lunch. If I don't, it's your treat!" I was a bit taken aback as I'd never been challenged like that before. But as I shook his hand I smiled and said, "You're on!"

Thirty days later, Wayde and I had a great lunch at his expense. Walking the talk of your values and creating a culture of accountability is a process, not an event. It isn't easy. We worked diligently to stay true to our values and encourage open and honest conversations. Some days we did well, other days not so much.

During an exit interview with an employee I was truly sad to see leave, I asked if she had any feedback on how we could improve. Her response was, "It's very hard to feel accepted here and to fit in. There are a lot of cliques and as a new person, I struggled to feel accepted."

That caught me off guard. As a manager, I should have been aware of the dynamic that was playing out every day. I hated to see her leave because was she was doing a great job. The lesson learned that day, that I carried with me for the next nine years was good performance doesn't always mean a happy employee. When employees are unhappy, their performance erodes over time or as in this case, they leave. Both are unacceptable outcomes and can be addressed with better employee engagement practices.

> ## Good performance doesn't always mean a happy employee.

When a company loses exceptional employees, the loss can be seen in three critical areas:

1. Impact on other employees
2. Impact on the bottom line
3. Impact on productivity

Managing people is hard work. In fact, there is nothing harder. Therefore, this critical aspect of running a company demands the leaders' time, demands systems that focus on helping employees be productive and demands that expectations are written down so everyone knows what is expected.

To keep exceptional employees and to reduce employee turnover, it's not enough for a company to just say that people are their greatest asset. They have to actually show they value their people. If a company is experiencing a high level of employee turnover, it isn't okay to dismiss it by thinking it was inevitable or that the employee wasn't that strong.

EXERCISE #1: FIND YOUR OWN SECRET SAUCE

The first sentence of Marcus Buckingham and Curt Coffman's best-selling book, *First Break All the Rules*, asks: What does a strong, vibrant workplace look like?

The authors devote a chapter to the story about a business owner, Stanley Lankford, and his three sons. Mr. Lankford founded his company in Ocean City, Maryland, back in 1964. In 1981, they merged with Sysco, the food distribution giant. Part of the agreement was that Mr. Lankford and all three of his sons would stay on in management positions.

In interviewing Mr. Lankford, Buckingham and Coffman learned that the Lankford-Sysco facility is in the top 25% of all of Sysco's facilities in growth, sales per employee, profit per employee and market penetration. They have single-digit turnover, absenteeism is at an all-company low and shrinkage is virtually nonexistent. And this facility consistently tops the customer satisfaction charts. How does this company do what so many other companies struggle to achieve?

The Lankfords use a pay-per-performance plan that measures everything. Every measurement is posted and every measurement has some kind of compensation attached. However, Mr. Lankford doesn't really feel these measurements really set his facility apart. The "secret sauce," he believes, is continual focus on the customer, highlighting the right heroes, treating people with respect and listening.

His company has 840 employees. Each one is engaged in what they do, they know why they do it and they know how it impacts the bottom line. They provide value every day. They are recognized for their performance and they thrill at the challenge of their work, and that's the real secret sauce!

I can hear the sigh of frustration now. Are you thinking about the employees you've tried to bring on board? Or how much time you spend with employees who aren't engaged and who don't perform to your standards? Are you thinking about projects that aren't profitable and people who aren't accountable? If you just had great employees, like Terri and Tom (insert your great employee name here) you could emulate great companies like Lankford-Sysco! Right? Oh, if it only were that simple.

You have to start with one small step, which will be a giant step for the good of your company. None of the success stories we read about are overnight successes. They all had to start with one small step. That's how you achieve greatness, and this is where management breaks down. No one wants to invest the time in setting up those performance measurements. No one has the time to think through a pay-for-performance program. Are you kidding? We have a company to run!

Here are three small steps that will immediately move your company from good to great when it comes to employee retention.

Discussion point #1: Articulate your philosophy about the people who work for you. Write down your answers to these five questions.

1. How do you want your employees to feel every day when they come to work?
2. What do you want them to believe in?
3. What do you want employees to know about your company?
4. How do you want them to treat each other?
5. How do you want your employees to treat your customers?

With up to 57 employees, this is the best time to commit to finding the secret sauce that will engage your employees, generate better profits and reduce your own burnout. Once you are clear on your answers to those five questions, ask each of your managers to answer them too. Better yet, answer them together as an exercise.

Discussion point #2: Working with your management team, determine:

- How will you communicate your philosophy of people to the employees in your organization?

- How will you reinforce employee commitment to the above?
- How will you address employees who challenge the above?

If you haven't created the core values that drive organizational behavior, make this a priority. Core values help employees make decisions that line up with your own beliefs. A template for creating your values can be found in my book, *The Art of Delegation: How to Effectively Let Go to Grow with 20 – 34 Employees.* Without a strong set of values, you are rudderless on a very choppy ocean.

Discussion point #3: Once you and your managers are clear on core company values, find out what makes each person tick. Every single employee needs to be able to identify the following:

1. What do they feel their strengths are? Are they doing work that plays to those strengths every day?
2. Does each employee know what's expected of them? Can they articulate their value to the overall goals of the company?
3. Does each employee have the equipment, materials and supplies they need to do their work?
4. In the last seven days, did they receive recognition or praise for doing something well?
5. Do they feel someone – their manager, the CEO – cares about them as a person?
6. Is there someone at work who encourages their development? Has someone talked to them about their own goals and aspirations?

So, what does a strong, vibrant workplace look like? The essence of a vibrant workforce can be felt when employees feel they are heard. They want to know someone actually cares about them. They want to know that what they do every day helps the company move forward. They want to believe their opinion matters. This is how you reduce employee turnover.

THE VALUE OF FINDING YOUR OWN SECRET SAUCE

As a COO, running a growing enterprise, I constantly read books on leadership and management. I was a part of a peer-to-peer advisory group of CEOs for 3½ years to learn from others and bring those ideas to my company. Here's the reality. A secret sauce is only as good as its ingredients. They have to make sense to you and they have to fit into the world you've created. More importantly, it has to be made up of what you are already very good at, with a little of this and a little of that mixed in. Only you know the proportions because you understand your business better than anyone else. Simply take components of the ideas that resonate with you, grab your team and your employees and stake out the time to create an approach everyone buys into.

EXERCISE #2: BE INTENTIONAL ABOUT REDUCING EMPLOYEE TURNOVER

Most employee turnover conversations happen when that exceptional employee walks into your office and announces he is leaving. Has that happened to you? Were you completely caught off guard?

At no time should the departure of an employee be a surprise. I've seen it happen countless times as I am working with CEOs. I'll get on a coaching call and the first thing they say is "John, our VP of Scheduling quit yesterday." My first response is: Were you surprised? To which the answer is usually "yes, he was doing such a great job, I'm totally amazed that he's leaving."

No one was having a dialogue with this employee. No one was paying attention to how they felt about their job. The employee probably felt abandoned, invisible and at the core of this issue was an inexperienced manager. Or a toxic manager.

4 STEPS TO REDUCE EMPLOYEE TURNOVER

In your company, do you regularly talk about employee turnover? Do you have an intentional plan on how to combat it? Are you engaged with your key managers regarding employee issues? Do you have a performance measurement that identifies your employee retention rate? Do managers get rewarded for keeping exceptional talent?

Follow these four steps to increase buy in and reduce turnover:

1. Introduce a One-on-One process to create a dialogue between a manager and an employee. To learn more about my One-on-One process, which I have used for years and require all of my clients to embrace, go to http://growasuccessfulbusiness.com/the-one-on-one-meeting and download my free report. This is a scheduled meeting between a manager and her direct reports, individually and on a weekly basis. The goal is to shift the focus from a manager-in-charge conversation to an employee-owned conversation. By shifting the focus to the employee, the barrier that commonly exists between a manager and an employee is removed, leading to much more authentic and meaningful conversations.

2. Promote and commit to an open-door culture where employees are encouraged to address problems and concerns without fear of reprisal. Start with yourself first and then focus on your managers. Are you suffering from the CEO Disease where no one is willing to tell you the truth – even those closest to you? When ideas come up that are different than yours or different from the way things have been done in the past, are you open-minded or do you get defensive? Is your first reaction to explain why what you are doing is right? Or do you let go of what you know and allow others to explore new ideas?

3. Create a results-focused culture where people know what's expected of them, know how to measure those results and are rewarded when results are met or exceeded. Don't try to eat the entire apple. Start with one-on-one conversations and help each person identify how their job impacts the bottom line. Ask each person to identify one or two key indicators that will help them know when they are being successful at their job. Ask them to map their key indicators to how meeting those milestones will help the overall company. You'll be surprised at how quickly people do this. And once people start seeing measurable results, you'll watch engagement improve.

4. Encourage a mentality that welcomes new ideas, creative solutions, and invites personal and professional learning. Think about the last time you were hosting a meeting and someone suggested a new idea. What was your reaction? Did you explain that "this wasn't the time," and "we need to focus on tasks at hand"? Did your body language suggest impatience at this interruption of a meeting with a critical agenda to get through? How do people in general react to something new? New ideas don't just pop up when you set aside a day long retreat and challenge people to think strategically about new markets, new partnerships, etc. Ideas and creative solutions occur in the moment when someone sees or experiences a new, better or different way to do

things. New ideas should be encouraged every day. And when an idea gets accepted and integrated, rewards should follow.

By simply applying these four steps, you'll be sending a strong message to everyone in your company that people are valued, their ideas are valued, and their contribution is valued.

THE VALUE OF BEING INTENTIONAL ABOUT REDUCING EMPLOYEE TURNOVER

When people that provide great performance, are a pleasure to work with, show respect and concern for others and understand and embrace the vision, mission and values of a company, you want them to stay. What is your overarching plan to make sure those exceptional people stay?

You need to find ways to understand what makes your employees tick; why they love working at your company; what would they like to see change; what they feel they do well. Your people ARE your business. Reducing employee turnover isn't something you think about when that next employee schedules 30 minutes of time with you and announces they are leaving. You should know the mindset of each and every employee and how they are feeling about their work on any given day.

A company's focus on training and developing strong leaders is the other link that ensures the longevity of employees a CEO wants to help build her business. Remember, people stay at a company because they respect their manager.

EXERCISE #3:
SET CLEAR EXPECTATIONS
AND MANAGE TO THOSE
EXPECTATIONS

Chuck Blakeman explains in his book, *Why Employees Are Always A Bad Idea*, that the concept of an employee was invented during the Industrial Age. The Factory System required people to run the machines. In 1911, Fredrick Winslow Taylor (to many the Father of the Management Process) wrote his definitive *Principles of Scientific Management*.

According to Blakeman, "Taylor's Scientific Management Theory was driven by two central and devastating assumptions: 1. Employees are stupid and 2. Employees are lazy." This Industrial Age way of thinking still permeates the business world today. I've actually had business owners express to me their belief that employees are stupid and lazy.

I read Blakeman's book after sharing the podium with him during a business forum in Denver, CO. I wish every business owner in the world (yes, *world*) would read his book and embrace every single idea he discusses because he hits the nail on the head. However, that won't happen, at least in my lifetime. I hope it will in yours.

In his book, Blakeman presents the concept of Stakeholders vs. employees, which is a forward thinking, well thought out and exceptionally valid idea. For instance, a Stakeholder requires leadership; an employee requires adult supervision. A Stakeholder is rewarded for results; an employee is rewarded for how long they stay at a company. Stakeholders focus on expanding their own competence; employees focus on their next promotion. A Stakeholder is concerned with finding meaning in their work; an employee believes in making money by working longer hours. A Stakeholder figures out how to do more than asked and figures out what isn't being done and does it; an employee waits to be told what to do.

Blakeman shares hundreds of examples of how the Stakeholder, community-focused concept works. Managers are not needed, which reduces employee turnover, and substantially increases employee engagement, revenues and profits. In Blakeman's Stakeholder scenario, the business owner shares the profits. Without a profit-sharing mentality, all of the concepts Blakeman advocates for above cannot work.

The idea of profit sharing, however, isn't new. In his book, *The Great Game of Business*, (published in 1994) Jack Stack introduced the concept of "open-book management." It was based on his experience as a Vice President at a large Fortune 500 company. He showed up to work one day and found out that the company was bankrupt. Vowing to never allow something like that to happen to him again, he started his own company. From the beginning, he brought Stakeholders on board and everyone knew everything about the finances of the startup. He was an early advocate for what is referred to today as "transparency."

Historically, it takes a lot for human beings to change behaviors and thought patterns. To Blakeman's point, the management concepts planted back in the early 1800s still drive many of our beliefs about leadership, management, managers, systems and processes. So, if you want to solve your employee turnover problem, stop reading this book and go buy Blakeman's book. Read it, and implement everything he talks about because his formula works.

Meanwhile, if you want to take a few baby-steps toward improving employee engagement and reducing employee turnover, I'll outline a few tried and true options. Effective communication is the underlying success factor in any situation. Discussion points will help stimulate conversations and open lines of communication throughout your organization.

WHAT IS YOUR MECHANISM TO GATHER EMPLOYEE INPUT?

Find a process to collect anonymous employee feedback. Why anonymous? I am not a proponent of anonymous surveys; I'm a proponent of a culture that encourages feedback on a daily basis and utilizes that feedback to make changes. However, because the statistics that tell us that employees are 71% disengaged on a regular basis, we primarily *do not* have cultures that support the type of daily, ongoing, in your face feedback that leads to real trust and communication. We have to try something else (anonymous feedback) to grow and get employees engaged.

Topics and suggested questions include:

Business Challenges

A list of the 27 Business Challenges uncovered in Fischer's research appears on page 19. Find out which challenges your employees think the company is faced with today and create your own assessment.

Get a read on how employees feel by having them rate these statements:

Growth

- I completely understand the growth strategy for our company.
- I believe our company has a winning formula for how to grow responsibly.
- I understand how my job duties directly relate to how the company makes and keeps money.
- The way we work is extremely well coordinated.
- The company's internal communication system is extremely effective.

Company Culture

- I have the right resources and tools to do my job.
- Everyone applies collective ideas when needed.
- I have the opportunity to do what I do best every day.
- We adapt our services to meet the customers' unique needs.
- Most of the decisions are made from the top down.
- Conflict is dealt with openly and effectively.

Staff Satisfaction

- I feel a strong sense of belonging to this company.
- I feel the company is strong financially.
- I feel a strong sense of trust with my teammates.
- When I have something to say, my manager listens.
- We learn from our mistakes.

As the COO for that marketing communications company, we took a much more in-depth Company Health Survey shortly after we had to lay off 30% of our staff due to the dotcom blowup of March 2000. Fear ran rampant, people were scared they would be the next to be laid off and productivity was almost at a standstill. Our managers were concerned that taking a health survey so soon after the layoffs was a waste of time. After all, did we really need a survey to ascertain how people were feeling?

We went ahead with the survey with our remaining team members. It was enlightening and extremely beneficial to learn that all of the assumptions we made going in – that everyone felt negatively about every aspect of the company – were 100% wrong.

The results showed we had a spirit-driven culture, which indicated people felt they were an important part of the company. They believed we supported creative thinking and that because we took care of our employees, they took care of the business. The results also showed that our company expectations were clearly communicated and understood. Our overall staff satisfaction rating was 4.15 out of 5.0.

By actually asking for staff feedback, we were able to take a positive direction based on their input and move forward.

Stop assuming. Start asking. Stop talking. Start listening.

EMPLOYEE ACCOUNTABILITY

Setting clear expectations is the employee's responsibility. An employee who sets their own expectations based on goals and performance plans is more likely to buy into those expectations. If a manager sets them, there is less buy in. Following up to ensure expectations are being met is the manager's responsibility.

Blakeman aptly points out in his book that managers tend to treat employees as children. Like children, we feel we have to hold their hand when they cross a street, or we have to teach them that the stove is hot. He likens the management approaches of today to the parent (the manager) telling the child (the employee) to go wash his hands for dinner. I agree. There is a tendency for managers to assume they have to be in charge; to think they are being paid to make decisions and improve results. This mentality sends a message to employees that managers "know more."

This management approach is buried deep into the psyche of so many organizations. It's ineffective and it creates the lack of accountability many companies suffer from every day. However, without embracing Blakeman's model (and again, I'm a fan), we have to work with where we are as organizations begin to shift the focus of accountability back to employees. In my experience, this works best when employees 1.) are aware of how their jobs impact the larger goals of the company and 2.) are given the responsibility to select and track their own key performance indicators.

A manager should simply support this effort and show interest in how well the employee is meeting those performance goals. Too often, managers force performance indicators onto employees who have no understanding of the "what" and even less understanding of the "why."

When expectations are poorly stated, poorly communicated and poorly tracked, the employees' frustration grows.

THE VALUE OF SETTING CLEAR EXPECTATIONS AND MANAGING TO THOSE EXPECTATIONS

"To be unclear is to be unkind." This quote by Dave Ramsey, personal financial guru, says it all. When you aren't setting clear expectations, and working with each and every employee on what that looks like, problems can become a crisis overnight. When you are starting with a toxic culture, employee engagement can be a long uphill climb.

I worked with a company for years that struggled with this concept. The leadership's constant complaint was "a lack of accountability." I met and talked with each and every employee during my work at the company and here were some of their concerns:

- Turnover is creating serious capacity issues.
- There is no agenda for meetings.
- I never know what materials are needed for a job.
- The website isn't up-to-date and doesn't showcase the company.
- No one takes ownership of their work.
- The equipment isn't kept clean.
- We're not using technology to our advantage.
- The commission payments take too long.
- We have great ideas but no one is listening.
- There is a lot of redundancy and wasted time in how work gets done.

These are challenging issues, absolutely, but they are not impossible to resolve. When I asked the employees if they had raised these issues with the leaders of the company, the response was, "they won't listen, they don't want to hear it. Even if we bring it up, nothing gets done." The constant sense of crisis was wearing the employees down. I watched good employees leave. Underperforming employees stayed, knowing, that if they just kept their heads down, they could continue to stick around.

When presented with these issues, leadership simply felt "people just needed to stop whining and do what they are paid to do." The leaders were burnt out, frustrated and looking for a silver bullet to solve their problems. I couldn't give them a silver bullet. All I could suggest was that we start with setting clear expectations and managing to those expectations.

To run a successful company, you have to set clear expectations and manage to those expectations and that involves managing people.

While thousands of books are written on leadership, management, and emotional intelligence every year, I believe some people are simply not meant to manage people. It's not in their nature and it's not good or bad. If you find yourself managing people and you are miserable doing it, stop. Get another job. If you are the CEO, fire yourself and put someone in your place that enjoys helping people succeed. While people are your business, you don't have to be the one who manages those people.

RESOLVING THE CHALLENGE OF EMPLOYEE TURNOVER

Retaining exceptional employees is the only way a business can capitalize upon profits, productivity and performance. The number one job for any leader is the development and management of people. Without them, there won't be a business to run.

The 2012 Bad Boss Study found that, in general, bosses leave their employees feeling unappreciated, uninspired, and downright miserable. Michelle McQuaid, a leader in the field of positive psychology, conducted interviews with a cross section of a thousand U.S. workers. She found:

- 64% of workers are unhappy in their job
- 31% of employees feel uninspired and unappreciated by their boss
- 15% are bored, lonely and miserable
- 42% say their boss doesn't work very hard
- 20% indicate their boss has little or no integrity
- 47% suggest their boss loses his or her cool under stress
- 73% of those in their 20s and 30s say their health is at stake because of their relationship with their boss
- 40% of those 50 and older feel the same
- Only 38% say their boss is great

A toxic environment is deadly to success. And the problem is twofold. Productive employees will leave those toxic environments, taking their critical skills elsewhere. The less than productive employees will stay.

Gallup studies also uncovered three types of employees:

Non-engaged employees: 56% of the US workforce falls into this category. These employees are neutral to the company's initiatives. They are not positive or negative about their company. These people show up most of the time and do only what is expected of them. They may not be actively looking for another job, but would have no problem leaving if another job presented itself. These employees have no company loyalty. Many times, these individuals started with the company as engaged employees but their engagement slipped over time. Non-engaged employees will not ask for extra work. They will only work the required hours; no overtime.

To re-engage these workers, their manager should have a real discussion with each employee privately. The manager should ask what they want out of their experience with the organization.

Managers need to find out if the employee has any ambition or desire to be promoted. Also, giving them work they enjoy that highlights their skills will help the process.

Engaged Employees: Engaged employees make up an average of 29% of the workforce. They are the bright spots in the organization. A successful company with outstanding performance numbers is made up primarily of highly engaged employees.

These people bring excitement, productivity and creativity to the office environment. Many times their attitudes are contagious to the non-engaged employees.

Leaders should be careful not to squelch their enthusiasm. Don't ignore them by thinking they don't need as much attention because they bring their own motivation. Engaged employees need reassurance and encouragement just as much as the non-engaged employees.

Give this group the opportunity to stretch their talents and skills, which will instill even more confidence. To have an engaged employee base, leaders must first have an organization that fosters trust in management, fair compensation and a positive company outlook.

Actively disengaged employees: 15% of the US workforce falls into this category. These employees are the most detrimental to the morale and success of the organization. They are extremely unhappy and they don't mind expressing their unhappiness openly in the office. Other employees may describe them as saboteurs or non-workers. When put on a team project, they will leave most of the work to their team members. If a company has too many disengaged employees, immediate personnel changes need to be made. These individuals can bring down the organization with their open toxicity.

Actively disengaged employees voice their complaints. Leaders should attempt to re-engage these employees by listening to their problems. Although leaders do not want to encourage dissension among their staff, the disengaged employees may have some valid points. Their complaints may lead to process improvements that could enhance the entire organization.

Of the three, the actively disengaged employees create the most damage. Do you know where your employees stand? Can you identify the difference? Are you paying as much attention to the engaged employees as you should, or are you giving all of your time to the actively disengaged employees?

Increase the number of engaged employees and profits will increase. What better reason do leaders have to focus critical resources on hiring, training and developing exceptional employees and reducing employee turnover?

In a recent article by Randall Beck and Jim Harter, on *Why Great Managers Are So Rare*, they site a Gallup study that finds great managers have the following talents:

- They **motivate** every single employee to take action and engage employees with a compelling mission and vision.
- They have the **assertiveness** to drive outcomes and the ability to overcome adversity and resistance.
- They create a culture of clear **accountability**.
- They build **relationships** that create trust, open dialogue, and full transparency.
- They **make decisions** based on productivity, not politics.

Beck and Harter assert that, "When companies can increase their number of talented managers and double the rate of engaged employees, they achieve, on average, *147% higher earnings per share* than their competition."

As the CEO of a growing enterprise, there is every reason in the world to take the time to hire, train and develop exceptional managers – this is your first line of defense against high employee turnover.

THE HIDDEN COSTS OF EMPLOYEE TURNOVER

Reduced productivity: Who is filling in to keep the work moving forward for the vacated position? It's not easy to farm out someone's task, it takes time to bring a newcomer up to speed and something is bound to fall through the cracks.

Remaining staff is overworked: Your existing team is already working hard. As people scramble to pick up vacated work, they are stretched even thinner. The result is their satisfaction goes down along with their work quality and engagement. The longer this goes on, the harder it will be to regain their goodwill, even after you have filled the position.

Lost knowledge: Even if other people can do what the former employee did, they don't have the specific knowledge that comes from experience. When someone's been at a company for some time, they know the people, how things really work, who to turn to for answers, where things are and the little efficiencies created over time. That knowledge goes away when someone leaves. In most cases, the tasks haven't been documented, processes aren't captured and cross training never took place.

Training costs: Typically, new hires require onboarding training. They may need to take a class or receive a certification. But even when there are no training classes to attend, someone has to train the new person on what to do. Someone has to double-check the work until the new person is up to speed, which takes that person away from her regular job, which means you are paying two people to do one job. Losing an employee, whether due to poor performance or for their own reasons, is hard for small companies: emotionally, financially and physically.

Financial Cost: Turnover is always expensive. The most tangible reason to decrease employee turnover can be felt on the bottom line. The costs to rehire can be as high as 150 percent of an annual salary.

• •

The benefits of reducing employee turnover:

- Eliminate the cost of hiring and training a new employee.
- Morale increases when employees feel good about where they work and people stick around.
- Employee retention attracts outside prospective talent.
- Increased operational output because employee exits and new hires are common work disrupters.
- If an employee joins the competitor, confidential information is in jeopardy.

The best offense is to create a company where employees feel valued, love coming to work and provide solid performance (because they track their key indicators). Those factors equate to a better bottom line, reduced employee turnover and increased engagement.

Challenge #4:
Not Able to Quickly
Get Systems and
Procedures in Place as
the Company Grows

To function effectively, a company must have day-to-day operations in place. This requires that leaders have a plan that outlines exactly what systems and procedures the company needs to grow. An important point to make as we explore this challenge is this: while systems and procedures are critical for sustainability and scalability, ignoring or not prioritizing skill development and training for your staff will sabotage your efforts. People want to be trained and given time to get used to the new systems. Their success relies on not getting the system in place, but being able to utilize the system effectively.

It's important to understand the nuances between the definitions of the following three concepts:

System: a group of interacting, interrelated or interdependent elements that form a complex whole; process is a synonym of system

Procedure: an established or official way of doing something; system is a synonym of procedure

Process: a series of actions or steps taken in order to achieve a particular end

I'll use the word "systems" to cover processes and procedures in order to simplify this discussion.

Putting procedures, processes and/or systems in place can seem overwhelming to young organizations. There is a strong tendency to ignore the need for more sophisticated systems, especially if the CEO is the specialist who created the product or service. Their belief is often, "if I could get a high volume of work out when it was just me and a few people, why can't we do the same today?"

When activity levels increase tenfold; leaders tend to throw people at the activity. The irony is that more people create a more complex organization that is more difficult to manage. As a result of throwing people at the problem, the company ends up in another stage of growth before it is ready. The necessary systems to build a suitable infrastructure have not yet been created.

It's much easier to decide something is a people issue than to determine it's a process issue. For example, if clients complain that it takes too long to hear back from someone when they lodge a complaint, the leader may assume the person in charge of customer service is at fault or overstretched. Usually, the quick fix thinking is to just hire another customer service person because it's a less expensive solution than implementing a CRM system.

As with many other aspects of growing a successful business, the CEO needs a plan. They need to know what systems are important for the company, and she won't know that unless she has run a similar type of company, looked for outside expertise or hired experienced managers who understand the problem.

Ask yourself:

- What systems do you currently need for your stage of growth?
- How do you define those systems and what exactly do you need them to do?
- Have you set aside money to purchase, maintain and upgrade critical systems?
- Have you planned time for training?
- How do you know the systems in place are efficient?
- Are any of the existing systems broken?

Ultimately you need a way to systemize how work gets done. In Chapter 5, I identified 14 Master Processes that are critical to sustain and scale growth. For Stage 4, there are three a company needs to pay attention to: Operations, Project Management and Production. This assumes, however, that as the company grew through Stages 1, 2 and 3, you have already addressed Financial, Sales, Marketing, Forecasting/Tracking, Communications, Human Resources and Work Community.

My own experience in the area of systems management within a growing company came down to learning the hard way. As is typical with a fast growing, small business, we never made thinking about systems a priority.

In Stages 1 and 2 (1 – 19 employees), with revenues of $1.9 million, we relied on "sneaker net." We passed documents back and forth, shared information in meetings, and expected people to keep track of issues and processes their own way. After all, we had made it this far using that approach, why would we change?

We had reached the point in our growth cycle that Doug Tatum describes as "No Man's Land" (in his book by the same name). Sales stagnate, employees grow more and more unhappy, you can't obtain credit and you wonder if you should just throw in the towel. You are working 12-hour days, 7 days a week. What you once thought was a great adventure has turned into a nightmare. The problems feel too big to be small and too small to be big. You are stuck, essentially, in No Man's Land. It's time for systems management.

At that stage in our growth, I was an employee. I was acting like a Chief Operations Officer but titles and positions were still very fluid. Even this early in our growth, it was apparent that our CEO was the WHAT person and I was all about the HOW. She could sell ice cream to Eskimos and I figured out how to deliver on her promises. I hadn't become an owner in the company but she and I worked well together as a team. My role was account manager, project manager, financial manager and human resources manager. She was the sales manager, financial manager, technical manager and account manager. Our roles merged and separated daily, which created confusion among our staff and clients.

In 1997, we moved from Stage 3 to Stage 4 (35 – 57 employees) and things went from bad to worse. An entry in one of my day timers in January of that year says, "In general, things are completely out of control." The CEO was out of town working with a large client and she called into the office daily. She spoke to whoever picked up the phone and issued orders for things to be done to help her client. She didn't go through our managers, didn't go through me; she just went directly to the employees and asked them to stop what they were doing and help her.

We didn't have systems or procedures in place to manage how workflow happened. We didn't prepare for the challenge of an involved owner not realizing her impact on that workflow daily.

The chaos this caused was impossible to manage. There were days I thought every single employee would walk out the door. Not to mention my frustration in reacting to every crisis, every minute of every day.

I had not met James Fischer yet and did not know about the 7 Stages of Growth. That chaos would have been far more manageable if I understood the dynamics of Stage 3 and 4 companies and their challenges.

My experience in moving through the stages of growth provides me with empathy for any and all leaders who are trying their best to navigate through this challenging stage of growth. My presentations focus on solving the challenges that raise their ugly heads in each stage of growth in order to provide that critical ability to "address the root cause of issues."

EXERCISE #1: IDENTIFY THE SYSTEMS YOU CURRENTLY NEED

Think systems, in addition to people, when dealing with growth issues in Stage 4. You need a process to handoff new customers your sales team just landed. If the CEO is still the sales person, this gets even more challenging.

In our case, the CEO was the main contact for any and all new and existing customers. As we transitioned to account managers, we needed to put a process in place to move the new customer to the account manager without the customer feeling abandoned. If you are in a manufacturing environment, you need a process to hand the sale off to a plant manager, or a floor supervisor, or a General Manager so that it can be scheduled into the existing work flow and the right machines and the right operators will be available.

Those processes need to work every day no matter who is there, which is the real test of a system. If the lead supervisor is sick, does workflow come to a grinding halt? Who is responsible for the process from beginning to end?

Who is responsible for documenting the process? Is it a plant manager, an account manager, a general manager? It doesn't need to be a 100-page document. You want to capture the process at a high level, not every single aspect of every single process. Capture the basic critical steps with several bullet points under each step, which are procedures. The employees simply need a general guideline to follow and the managers need a reference point to double check that critical steps weren't being missed or ignored.

By Stage 4, a company should have seven of the 14 Master Processes already in place. Don't worry. It's all manageable IF you take it seriously, allocate funds to identify, develop and capture the key systems, and engage every single person in your company to help. Start now.

I highly recommend you first identify your core processes by name, take the first stab at outlining how they currently work. Figure out what works for your company, test each one to see that it's effective and then, if you need further assistance in upgrading to a more sophisticated and technologically-efficient approach, you can. Knowing what works for your company can save a lot of money and time when you bring on an outside resource.

THE VALUE OF IDENTIFYING THE SYSTEMS YOU CURRENTLY NEED

Systems make your operations more efficient and the company more profitable. They also help your employees enjoy coming to work every day.

I have found that employees love processes, systems and procedures because they lead to greater efficiency. Processes mean they don't have to "figure it out" along the way. Your employees want to know how to do their job well. They want to succeed and documented processes tell them when things have gone well.

If you have a culture that encourages people to speak their minds, jump right in. Ask for input on how you can improve the way you work. Ask for solutions. If you have a culture that hasn't encouraged people's input or people's input is ignored or unsolicited, take a step back and implement some procedures that show people you care about what they say.

EXERCISE #2: CHALLENGE EVERY SINGLE PERSON IN THE COMPANY TO BE A SYSTEMS THINKER

How often have you sat down with the front-line staff and asked: *What one improvement could we make to our project management system that would make your life easier?*

Or how about: *If you were the CEO for a day, what immediate change would you make in how we manage our work processes?*

Or: *Given there were no limitations on resources, what one change would you make that would improve how we get work done?*

If you want to take on the challenge of not being able to get systems in place as the company grows, talk to the people who run your business every day.

Set up weekly round table discussions to encourage people to talk about what's working well and what needs to be improved. This very simple approach is seldom implemented for one (and only one) reason. "We don't have time!"

Right. But you have all the time in the world to redo work, shore up mistakes, pay for overtime, pay for extra shipping charges, discount projects that are late, and the list goes on and on.

If you are a Stage 4 CEO and feel like the wheels are coming off your company (I've been there), I will tell you it's because you still think you have all the answers. I will tell you it's because you aren't tapping into the intelligence of your people. I will tell you it's because you are making faulty assumptions that your people aren't good enough, aren't committed enough or don't know enough.

For your own sanity, stop and engage. Show people that what they have to contribute is important and that you care about what they have to say. Don't sugar coat the issues. If profits are eroding, show them where. Then help them understand how they can help. If customer complaints are increasing, give real examples. Then ask your staff what they would do to fix that issue. If shipments are consistently late, or inventory issues are impacting production schedules, ask for ideas on what can be done to fix it.

Leaders and managers need to adopt the attitude: "we can solve any problem if we all work together."

THE VALUE OF CHALLENGING EVERY SINGLE EMPLOYEE TO BE A SYSTEMS THINKER

When the entire company is focused on making the product or service the best it can be, exceeding customer expectations and creating sustainable profit margins, you're well poised to succeed. If you allow ineffective systems to continue because you don't feel you can take the time to evaluate this critical aspect of your company, skinny back down to a one or two-person company and have a great time!

If you want to continue to grow your company, provide exceptional service to your customers and be the leading provider in your industry, then you need to make systems thinking a part of your culture. It isn't hard. It just takes time, focus and commitment. Start small. Start somewhere. Start now.

RESOLVING THE CHALLENGE OF NOT BEING ABLE TO QUICKLY GET SYSTEMS AND PROCEDURES IN PLACE AS THE COMPANY GROWS

The CFO of Starbucks, Orin Smith, reached out to a well-known consulting firm when the company was ramping up for growth. He wanted the firm to help them move from an entrepreneurial to a well-managed company. He thought the biggest challenge would be getting Howard Schultz, the CEO and founder of Starbucks, to buy into the concept. Smith cautioned the consulting firm that Schultz might not have the patience for processes and systems. He was wrong.

Schultz fully embraced the changes the consulting firm proposed. They were consistent with his belief that if you're going to build a large building, you need a strong foundation.

The move to more systems, more processes and more procedures can be a hard transition for many entrepreneurs to embrace. However, it's never too early to think about what systems you need to create a foundation for growth.

When Tom Peters wrote the first edition of *Thriving on Chaos*, twenty-nine years ago, one of his critical principles was: "The need for flexibility in an increasing complex environment requires systems to be less complex and inevitably, we measure the wrong things."

Peters encouraged leaders to pay attention to what was going on in the trenches and engage the staff, who run those systems every day, to suggest improvements. They need to hold themselves accountable for the outcomes. If you've shared the company's larger vision and goals, the staff knows how what they do every day fits into that picture. All of Peters' insights still hold true today.

Start by having some critical conversations with your employees. Ask for their help with the following questions:

- Are we making assumptions that systems and procedures work?
- What can we stop doing? What should we start doing?
- Do we make it easy for changes to be made to existing systems?
- Can we describe what a good system or an effective procedure looks like?
- How are we rewarded for improvements to processes?
- How does our culture encourage or discourage change and flexibility?

Systems don't run themselves. People run them. Make your systems user friendly, instead of forcing employees to struggle with unfriendly, outdated, inefficient systems.

Challenge #5: Organization Needs to Understand How the Company Will Grow in the Future

How big do we have to get?" I started hearing this question when we grew from 5 to 12 people in a little over 9 months. It wasn't a question based in curiosity; it was a question laced with pain.

We were growing quickly, adding new people to a very small, family-like atmosphere and people were not happy. We moved out of the business owner's basement, into our first office space and took on a five-year lease. Our revenues had grown 67% and our staff grew by 140%. Life, as we had known it for two years, changed, seemingly overnight and we were far from prepared to handle it.

Our formula for helping people cope with long hours, chaotic procedures, lack of systems, and lack of clarity in job duties was to pay them well, provide lots of fun perks (dinners with spouses, tickets to basketball games, Friday pizza and beer parties) and try to convince them that growing was a good thing: more sales, better salaries, better equipment, etc.

I didn't have the insight then that the 7 Stages of Growth now provides business owners. In hindsight, I can see how being able to put a name to our pain would have helped. We didn't know, for instance, that we had just experienced a Flood Zone – where the level of activity increases and you feel like you are drowning. We didn't help our staff understand that we were "destabilized by chaos" and that was typical for our stage of growth. We knew we had to increase sales to pay for all the new overhead and salaries but we didn't understand the challenge we would face getting our services ready to market. That had everything to do with the fact that we really didn't have a plan for growth.

This challenge of *understanding how a company will grow* creates more obstacles than any of the other challenges of growth. Clarity of purpose and a clear perspective of what the company does should be at the forefront of the leader's communication with employees as often as possible. Any confusion or uncertainty as to exactly what the company does, what it delivers, to whom and why needs to be addressed and explained now!

EXERCISE #1: IDENTIFY TALENT AND SKILLS NEEDED TODAY FOR FUTURE GROWTH

The second call came a week after the first call. I had already explained to the person on the other end of the line that we weren't hiring right now. When she called back a week later, I was a bit surprised and slightly irritated. I thought, "Now what?"

The woman on the line was the Creative Director for a large advertising agency in New York. By the time I hung up the second time, I had agreed to a face-to-face meeting. She was going to be in the area the following week, as her husband was being transferred to Boulder, CO (where our company was located) and she had called back to see if she could stop by for a visit.

That unintentional meeting led to one of the most strategic and beneficial hires I have ever made. During our first "interview," she explained why we needed her. She had followed our growth from a distance and even though creatively we were considered one of the best shops around, she could take us to the next level. She delivered on that promise.

As I reflect back on my hesitation in making this critical hire, I was worried about how I would handle someone with her experience. It's human nature to be a bit intimidated by someone who knows more than you. I was also worried about the salary we would have to pay her. Could we afford it? What kind of precedence would it set?

All of my fears evaporated as I witnessed an experienced manager in action. During our interview, she told me that her philosophy was to manage with her head and her heart. When she started to work with her team, I watched her define each person's role and responsibilities. She had to let some people move on and I was impressed with the new hires she brought in. She defined creative standards. She set up systems and evaluated processes. She threw out the things that stopped people from succeeding and embraced and improved the things that were working.

The talent and skills you need as a Stage 4 company are different than what you needed when you had 10 employees. Have you fundamentally and intentionally changed your recruiting and hiring practices and/or your interviewing processes from when you had fewer employees? Are you assuming that the same skills and talent that got you where you are now will take you to the next level?

To answer that question, you need to know where you are going as a company. CEOs should ask their managers and managers should ask their staff:

- Can you describe the company's core competencies?
- What business are we in?

Leader may be shocked when people respond by listing what they do for the company and further shocked to realize that the company's core competency and purpose is lost on most employees.

Up until 1900, human knowledge doubled approximately every century. By World War II, it doubled every twenty-five years. Today our knowledge is doubling every 12 – 18 months. This just underscores the need to be aware of what knowledge, skills, talent and information your business needs to ensure you don't fall behind the competition.

Engage your entire company to answer four critical questions:

1. Are we keeping up with our growth? Why or why not?
2. Do we encourage self-directed learning and support people learning new skills and gaining new knowledge to remain valuable assets?
3. Do we know what new skills and knowledge we want people to acquire and why?
4. Are we setting aside resources to help people learn new skills?

THE VALUE OF IDENTIFYING TALENT AND SKILLS NEEDED TODAY FOR FUTURE GROWTH

By first understanding where the company is going and then by addressing what skills and talents the company needs to get there, a CEO is better positioned to make good hiring decisions.

Leaders need to make it a point to tap into the intelligence of the organization on a regular basis. Find out how employees view the company, the leadership of the company, its customer service, its products, the culture, the core values, what skills they feel the company needs and how they feel they are helping the company stay ahead of the competition.

As a company moves into Stage 4, the CEO will be challenged every day in areas she needs help with. Recognizing the areas that need to be strengthened starts with a CEO who isn't afraid to hire and bring on talent with different skills, different experiences and diverse backgrounds.

EXERCISE #2: STOP LETTING GROWTH BECOME A SIX-LETTER WORD

Growth is scarier for employees than it likely is for a CEO or an entrepreneur. To help your organization understand how growth will impact the company, start by helping employees understand how growth will impact them. You have to break down the challenges of growth in a way that each and every person in your company gets. In order to engage employees in your growth plan, they have to see how they fit into that future.

Leaders should not assume that just because they know something, their employees know it as well. Don't assume managers are taking the critical messages back to their teams and sharing that information with their employees.

Despite our best intentions, our messaging can still backfire. Consider the following:

> You say: We're pursuing new opportunities.
> Employee thinks: Here we go again!

> You say: We're all in this together.
> Employee thinks: She has no clue what I do!

You say: According to our strategic plan ...
Employee thinks: I have no clue what she does!

You say: This will be a win-win for everyone!
Employee thinks: I'm tired of not getting paid what I'm worth!

You say: I just need you to get on board!
Employee thinks: Can't she see I'm working all the time?

You say: We're taking the company to the next level.
Employee thinks: How big do we have to get?

Growth quickly becomes a six-letter word that drives employees to shut down, deny and disengage. I refer to this reaction as growth trauma: when the very act of growing puts so much pressure on the organization that no one sees the impact until it is much too late. If no one talks about the changes that are coming, growth trauma will impact all aspects of your organization. It occurs slowly and builds to a crescendo when good employees walk out the door because they are frustrated, burned out, or angry because they keep working harder with no end in sight.

Symptoms of growth trauma:

- Low voltage (energy)
- High staff turnover
- Prevalent gossip
- Drop in sales and profits
- Growing customer service problems
- Loss of confidence and trust

What symptoms are you experiencing today? I've shared many examples of how growth trauma showed up in our marketing communications company. Our issue was we didn't know what we didn't know. The Stages of Growth model provides headlights into the future so a business owner can literally look ahead and get prepared for what they know is coming.

Growth can be managed. It's your choice to address it or ignore it. In our case, we had to get out of our own way and tap into our employee's intelligence. Solutions showed up quicker, problems didn't become as challenging and people stepped up and took responsibility for helping us grow when we recognized the intelligence inside each individual who worked with us. It wasn't an easy lesson to learn, and many people paid the price for my business partner and my unwillingness to listen better, ask more questions and set clear expectations.

I have always admired Zig Ziglar, the great author and motivational speaker, and was fortunate to have met him just months before he passed away. His presence on stage, even when he needed help to walk up the stairs, was impressive and captivating. His passion for helping people never faltered.

One of Mr. Ziglar's quotes that I use often when working with business owners is, "Encouragement is the fuel on which hope runs." At breakfast at that same conference, this wonderful man shared, "it's such an easy thing to supply, encouragement." He talked about the impact of a kind word, the power of a pat on the back for a job well done and how rewarding it was to see someone smile. Small steps make for large gains.

Healing growth trauma in your organization starts with creating open dialogue and ends with helping people see the value they bring to the organization.

> Small steps make for large gains.

Consistently applied, these five small steps will help your organization heal growth trauma and stay ahead of your growth curve.

1. **Share Your Thoughts** – Your employees want to know what you are thinking, how you feel about specific things and how you view the world they work in every day.

2. **Ask for Their Input** – Your employees are smart, capable and motivated people so take the time and look for opportunities to ask their opinions. Find out what they think about their job and how it impacts the overall company.

3. **Provide Clear Direction** – Don't make your people guess what you want or how you want it done by taking the attitude, "they should already know."

4. **Show Their Impact** – Track key indicators that have been created and embraced by each and every employee and share those results daily.

5. **Encourage Innovation** – Encourage people to think about and to explore different ways of doing things, and help them see the impact those ideas have on the organization.

THE VALUE OF NOT LETTING GROWTH BECOME A SIX-LETTER WORD

With up to 57 employees, growth is critical to the sustainability of your company. How you define growth, how you talk about growth, how you engage your employees in that conversation about growth is the critical component to not allowing GROWTH to become a six-letter word.

After our staff revolution (which I talk about in my Stage 3 book), we started asking our staff a question that served us well as we grew larger:

What issues are you dealing with today that you didn't have yesterday?

We asked it in company meetings and at management meetings. We had our managers ask it in their department meetings, and it became a part of the manager/employee one-on-one weekly meetings.

We asked this question to find out two things:

1. What isn't changing that should?
2. What is changing that shouldn't?

Think about it. This simple question could uncover a process that worked yesterday but is no longer relevant. The fact that it's become irrelevant may be why profits are eroding, customers are unhappy, and/or employees are frustrated. Or you may find something that has been lost along the way: a specific meeting that is no longer being held or an event that was canceled that brought people together. Sometimes reinstating an older process or practice makes all the difference in the world.

The main reason GROWTH becomes a six-letter word is we allow it to be the elephant in the room. Let growth to be a part of your everyday conversations, instead of a dreaded six-letter word.

EXERCISE #3: BE INTENTIONAL AND INSPIRATIONAL IN YOUR COMMUNICATIONS

I constantly remind my audiences that I could solve 90% of all problems CEOs experience in running their companies if I could simply get people to communicate more often, more consistently and more effectively. I think that starts with an intentional communications plan that defines what needs to be communicated, to whom, when and how will it be communicated. (Refer back to Challenge #2, Exercise #3 on how to create an intentional communications plan.) Surprisingly enough, these are few and far between. I further believe that if CEOs focus on providing intentional and inspirational communications when that first employee is hired, we'd start to change the statistic that only 20% of all small businesses survive their first five years.

I love this definition of communication:

To transmit *information*, *thoughts* or *feelings* ...

... so that they are *satisfactorily received* or *understood.*

And what I particularly enjoy is the last part that talks about those communications being satisfactorily received or understood.

How often do you, as the leader of an organization, ask this question after delivering your monthly financial report, or talk about the new contract you just landed?

"How many of you understood what I just said?"

In a culture where people are encouraged to speak their mind, share their thoughts openly and ask inquiring questions, you may get a good showing of hands. It's not the people who raise their hands that should impress you. It's the people that don't raise their hands that you need to follow up with.

In a culture where asking questions, challenging beliefs and stirring up the status quo isn't the norm, all hands will go up because people will be afraid and ashamed to admit otherwise. The challenge isn't transmitting information, thoughts or feelings. The challenge is how satisfactorily received or understood they are.

This quote by Margaret Miller says it all: "Most conversations are simply monologues delivered in the presence of a witness."

How many monologues are you having every day in your organization? Are you willing to take your communications to a whole new level and challenge your managers and employees to do the same?

Make a commitment to be more intentional and inspirational about your communications. Don't assume people know something and never assume they don't want to know something. Find out what your employees care about. What do they want to know more about? What information do they feel is missing that if they knew more, they could make better decisions?

Start by asking:

What needs to be communicated?

Who needs to know what, when?

Your administrative assistant needs to know different things than your lead supervisor on the plant floor. However, everyone needs to understand how their job impacts the bottom line. Everyone needs to be aware of policies and procedures that impact how the company operates safely and efficiently.

How often do you have to communicate?

Do you think that talking about your financials once a month teaches your employees to care about profit? Think again. Help each employee understand how what they do every day, impacts the company's bottom line. Find ways to help them draw a direct line from their job to the company's ability to be profitable. This doesn't have to be about Open Book Management (OBM) popularized by Jack Stack in his best-selling book, *The Great Game of Business,* where all financial information is shared with everyone, including salaries. Start with small steps. Find ways to teach financial literacy to your employees so they start to understand concepts like:

- The difference between cash and revenue.
- How their job helps generate profit for the company.
- The top three most expensive items on a profit and loss statement.
- The correlation between company success and exceptional customer service.
- Helping customers link their success to your products and services.

- How sales revenues minus cost of goods sold equal gross profit.
- How changes in inventory impact your cost of goods sold.

By simply helping employees better understand the "business of running a business," they become more engaged in helping the company reach its goals. If they see a direct correlation between what they do every day and how the company improves profitability, they will start thinking more as a shareholder, not just an employee.

THE VALUE OF BEING INTENTIONAL AND INSPIRATIONAL IN YOUR COMMUNICATIONS

As outlined in Challenge #2, creating an intentional communication plan is essential. You must find ways to communicate critical information daily, to the right people, at the right time. How you deliver it, must meet the standard of "inspirational." How can you be inspirational about a month when you lose money? What's the inspirational message in layoffs? Inspirational isn't about everything going well. Inspiration can be found in good news and not so good news. It's all in how the person sending the message is perceived.

When my business partner and I had to lay off 30 people to avoid bankruptcy, our focus was singularly directed toward putting a finger in the dam to staunch the flood of expenses cascading out of our company. We left little time to communicate what was happening to the rest of the staff. Our wake-up call came one morning when my administrative assistant let me know that people were confused, angry, hurt and living every day in fear that more layoffs were coming.

Inspiration was the last thing on my mind as we gathered everyone together for the first time since the layoffs. My business partner and I had spent several days thinking about what we could say about the future and how we would say it. She went first.

Her message was short and to the point. She said, "We are in trouble. We made some serious financial mistakes that led us here. We are taking steps to fix it. And our belief is, we will get through this." She didn't hide the fact that she was emotional and felt horrible about having to let people go. The first question she fielded was "will there be any more layoffs?" Her honest answer was "we aren't sure." She quickly followed that up by outlining the plan we had talked about. That plan included:

- Daily sales meetings to determine sales opportunities and discuss pipeline updates.
- Daily conversations with people who owed us money to try and recapture any and all receivables.
- The management team would take a 20% cut in pay on top of the 10% cut in pay they had already taken.
- No expenses would be approved without our controller's input and our final approval.
- Daily financial updates to track profits.
- We were working closely with our banker to manage our credit line and so far, they were being supportive and believed in our ability to weather the storm.

I then took the stage with the message that we needed each and every person in the company to be on top of their projects. I talked about how the better we manage each and every project, the more money we would keep. This meant staying on top of our billable hours, being efficient with our time and managing projects so we could invoice quickly in order to improve cash flow. I mentioned our goal was to avoid having to let anyone else go. I asked for questions and input and got an earful. But we also heard ideas on what each person could do to help. We heard people expressing their desire to help us succeed. Several people offered to take pay cuts (they said we should consider all employees, not just the management team to take pay cuts) instead of having to lay off any other employees.

At the end of the meeting, people came up and thanked us for sharing the information we did. They were glad to hear we had a plan and anxious to do their part. They thanked us for being honest, for not pretending things were okay. I believe what people heard that day was inspirational because it gave them hope. It gave myself and my business partner hope that people were on board, they understood the situation and they wanted to help.

I believe that the secret to effective communications, personal and professional, relies on intentional and inspirational communications.

What makes it Intentional?
- Having a plan
- Being consistent
- Knowing what to communicate to whom, when
- Not giving up

What makes it Inspirational?
- Transparency
- Authenticity
- Clarity
- Redundancy

Evaluate your communications today and ask yourself if by being more intentional you could change how people view your company. If you could inspire just one or two people a day, how that would impact your company?

RESOLVING THE CHALLENGE OF UNDERSTANDING HOW THE COMPANY WILL GROW IN THE FUTURE

Take the fear out of growth. Teach each and every person in your company how their job impacts the bottom line. Make growth a topic of conversation. Find consistent opportunities to share growth stories and experiences with your staff. Have people talk about their involvement in an activity that led to growth. Make growth conversations the norm and see how quickly employees embrace the goals of the company.

Start by answering these questions:

- Can you describe your company's growth plan?
- How do you communicate that plan to employees?
- How often has the company conducted a company health survey to ascertain how employees feel about the company?
- What mechanisms are in place to help the CEO communicate on a regular basis the goals and challenges of the company?

Work the growth conversation into the different layers of your organization:

1. COMPANY FOCUSED:

- What are our top 3 challenges today?
- Who are our top 3 competitors today?
- What is our growth strategy?
- What do we do well?
- How do we improve profitability?

2. TEAM FOCUSED:

- What is our mission?
- How does our work impact the company's bottom line?
- How can we improve our processes?
- How can we improve customer satisfaction?

3. INDIVIDUAL FOCUSED:

- What did you do last week that you're proud of?
- What can you learn next week to improve yourself and the company?
- How can I help?

The CEO of a company lives in the world she created every day. She knows exactly what she is doing and why. She has discussions with herself all the time about how well things are going or where the problems are or what can be done better.

If the CEO spends more time sharing these thoughts with employees and tapping into their perspectives, communication improves. When employees feel that their input is important and they are listened to, they stay engaged. More importantly, they see how their job fits into the overall goals of the company. The leaders can't assume employees know how the company will grow.

The CEO needs to be prepared to answer questions such as:

- How big are we going to get?
- Can't we just stay this size?
- Do we have to take on more work?

In their book, *The Founder's Dilemma*, authors Chris Zook and James Allen, share the following insight:

> The skills that help founders get their company to take off also are the opposite of those needed to sustain new growth. Founders focus on speed, ignore good process, and relish breaking the rules of the industry they are trying to disrupt. They cut corners, ignore detractors, and avoid naysayers. Their Herculean efforts are responsible for the firm's creation, but also its chaos. Once the company reaches cruising altitude, its leaders need to listen more to competing voices and invest more time in emerging stakeholders.

> One of these is what we called the unscalable founder. We believe the founder's mentality is a strategic asset. Nurtured correctly, it can help a company achieve scale insurgency - a company with the benefits of both size and agility. But many individual founders aren't scalable. Individual founders can become a barrier to growth if they are unable to let go of

the details and micromanage, or fail to build a cohesive team around them, or allow hubris to get in their way. We found 37% of executives at growing companies described the unscalable founder as a major barrier to their success.

In short, to borrow the title of Marshall Goldsmith's book, "what got you here won't get you there." Making the transition from entrepreneur to CEO is critical - and the same for the rest of the senior leadership team.

The impact of growth hits employees hard. Leaders need to help them understand the "why" of growth so they can see it as a positive and not something to be feared. When a company consistently finds out what employees think and shares results so employees can see changes occur based on their input, many beneficial outcomes occur.

1. Employees become more open to giving their opinions.
2. Employees become better observers of what the company is doing well and what it struggles with.
3. Employees gain a better understanding of what it really takes to run a successful company.
4. Everyone hears firsthand what the issues are, based on an objective system of gathering data.

To help employees understand how the company will grow in the future, tap into the many tools provided within the Stages of Growth framework. Take the time to explain what it means to be a Stage 4 company and what the typical issues a company of that size experiences. Explain the challenges. Describe the Wind Tunnel and the Flood Zone. Let them know what leadership styles you are focusing on to see the company through this stage. The value of understanding a company's growth curve is that it provides a language of growth, which takes the fear out of growing.

> *"Communication works for those who work at it."*
>
> *-John Powell*

What's Next?

The great thing about understanding your challenges upfront is that you can work on them immediately and move on! You don't have to worry about where to devote your time and you have a clear outline of how to move your company from Stage 4 with 35 - 57 employees to Stage 5 with 58 - 95 employees. As a leader of a Stage 4 organization, you have made it through some critical adjustments regarding your own leadership skills and are ready to put those to even greater use as you move into Stage 5.

Business owners who have the ability to focus on the right things at the right time build successful businesses. If you make sure that you are working on these five challenges every day, your company will respond and reward you with results.

Many business owners are not able to put words to their issues. They simply know there are issues hitting them every day and they *react* to each issue separately, depending upon how critical the issue is at that exact day and hour. Reacting to issues is not an effective way to grow a business. Understanding your key issues, identifying them and working on them is a formula for success!

As a company grows, so must the leader. Each stage of growth will require something different. Understanding what is required of you as your company evolves can either propel the company forward or cause the company to stagnate:

> As a company grows, so must the leader.

profits never materialize, sales suffer and there is high employee turnover.

"Managing the Managers" is the name of the game in a Stage 4 company. As you move closer to Stage 5 (58 – 95 employees) the priority shifts to bringing those managers together as a cohesive, decision-making team that is truly responsible for the success of the company. Now you have moved beyond 50 employees. Stage 5 is about integration and helping sales and marketing understand the issues with product development. Customer service is integrated into every aspect of your organization and as the CEO, you are operating with a proactive, systematic approach instead of a reactive, scattered approach.

> The complexity of an organization will always extract its due.

FOUNDATION BUILDING BLOCKS FOR A STAGE 4 COMPANY WITH 35 – 57 EMPLOYEES

Stage 4 brings a new set of challenges to the table. Here is a quick look at what you may be experiencing.

AREA	DESCRIPTION
Employees	You have 35 to 57 employees (you have breached the challenging "50" mark!)
CEO/Founder	Your role now is to manage your managers; to help them become confident and capable in their roles and responsibilities. You can't take your eye off the ball, however. The company needs your experience, your vision and your insight. Your goal is to help facilitate learning and development in your managers.
Team	You have 6 to 10 managers. They are trying hard to assert their own ideas and insights into their division. Let them. With your input. With a Coaching leadership style, not a Commanding Style. Help them become great managers.
Business Model	Examine everything surrounding your ability to make and keep money. Your overhead is expanding. Make sure you are ready for new costs and more expensive people.
Climate	There is a lot of: (a) confusion due to lack of company-wide clarity on who is responsible for what; (b) uncertainty about who has authority for what; and (c) tension in the air as you and the organization are being stretched.
Systems	Focus attention on systems and procedures. Make sure you are budgeting for upgrades where needed.
Cash	Cash flow should be well managed by now. Systems are in place to track inventory, labor and billable hours, and efficiency measures to protect cash and profit.
Focus	Your role is to stay on top of your managers and their goals and responsibilities. You need to ensure that they understand and are bought into your culture, vision, mission and values.

A STAGE 4 COMPANY AT A GLANCE

ENTERPRISE-CENTRIC

Number of Employees	35 - 57
Number of Managers	6 - 10
Number of Executives	2 - 3
Builder/Protector Ratio	3:2

Three Gates of Focus	Process
	Profit/Revenue
	People

3 Faces of a Leader	Visionary 10%
	Manager 70%
	Specialist 20%

Leadership Style	Primary – Coaching
	Secondary – Affiliative
	Auxiliary – Pacesetting

Leadership Competencies	Adaptability
	Organizational Awareness
	Service
	Developing Others
	Teamwork and Collaboration

Critical Processes for Stage 4   Project Management

                                        Operations

                                        Production

Critical Activities for Stage 4   Profit plan is set up

                                        Key indicators created by managers

                                        More emphasis on accountability

ARE YOU READY FOR STAGE 5 - INTEGRATION?

The 7 Stages of Growth has helped thousands of business owners focus on the right things at the right time. The framework helps business owners to uncover the root cause of an issue and then resolve that issue quickly.

As a Stage 5 company, you have 58 – 95 employees. The company is beginning to become integrated. Sales and marketing understands and is involved with product development. The company must start integrating teams and processes.

Customer service is tied into every aspect of your operation. As the CEO, you are operating in a proactive, systematic approach instead of a reactive, scattered approach. You have trained and/or hired qualified managers and their divisions are operating on solid ground.

Your skills as a manager are more critical than ever. You want to encourage autonomy in your managers while making sure they protect and maintain the culture and the values the company has developed over the years.

Are you ready to tackle the Stage 5 challenges? My book, *Foster Team Alignment: How to Cultivate Collaboration with 58 – 95 Employees*, offers tips on how to address the top five challenges for the fifth stage of growth. It will be available on Amazon.com in mid-2018.

"Laurie Taylor's books are an impressive distillation of learnings from the analysis of over six-hundred companies. Succinct and easily navigated, these books will stimulate your thinking about growth, profitability and staff."

-Steve Wylie
Chairman, Double You Solutions

You can order any of Laurie's books on the Stages of Growth at Amazon.com.

Survive and Thrive: How to Unlock Profits in a Startup with 1-10 Employees.

Sales Ramp Up: How to Kick Start Performance and Adapt to Chaos with 11-19 Employees.

The Art of Delegation: How to Effectively Let Go to Grow with 20-34 Employees.

Managing the Managers: How to Accelerate Growth through People and Processes with 35-57 Employees

Foster Team Alignment: How to Cultivate Collaboration with 58 – 95 Employees

ADDITIONAL RESOURCES

Blakeman, Chuck: *Why Employees Are Always a Bad Idea*

Bossidy, Larry: *Execution: The Art of Getting Things Done*

Buckingham, Marcus and Coffman, Curt: *First Break All the Rules*

Crabtree, Greg: *Simple Numbers, Straight Talk, Big Profits!*

Culbert, Samuel A.: *Good People, Bad Managers: How Work Culture Corrupts Good Intentions*

Dotlich, David and Cairo, Peter: *Why CEOs Fail*

Feld, Brad: *Startup Life: Surviving and Thriving in a Relationship with an Entrepreneur*

Fischer, James: *Navigating the Growth Curve: 9 Fundamentals that Build a Profit-Driven, People-Centered, Growth-Smart Company*

Flamholtz, Eric G. and Randle, Yvonne: *Growing Pains: Transitioning from an Entrepreneurship to a Professionally Managed Firm*

Fleury, Robert: *The Small Business Survival Guide*

Gerber, Michael: *The E-Myth; The E-Myth Revisted*

Goleman, Daniel; Boyatzis, Richard and McKee, Annie: *Primal Leadership: Realizing the Power of Emotional Intelligence*

Harnish, Verne: *Mastering the Rockefeller Habits; Scaling Up: How a Few Companies Make It and Why the Rest Don't*

Helfert, Erich: *Techniques of Financial Analysis: A Guide to Value Creation*

Keller, Scott and Meaney, Mary: *Leading Organizations: Ten Timeless Truths*

Ludy, Perry: *Profit Building: Cutting Costs without Cutting People*

Maxwell, John C.: *The 21 Irrefutable Laws of Leadership*

Peters, Tom: *Thriving on Chaos: Handbook for a Management Revolution*

Pfeffer, Jeffery: *Leadership BS: Fixing Workplaces and Careers One Truth at a Time*

Price, Ron and Lisk, Randy: *The Complete Leader*

Scott, Susan: *Fierce Leadership, Fierce Conversations*

Sherman, Andrew J.: *The Crisis of Disengagement: How Apathy, Complacency, and Selfishness Are Destroying Today's Workplace*

Sinek, Simon: *Start with Why*

Slywotsky, Adrian: *The Profit Zone; The Art of Profitability*

Stack, Jack: *A Stake in the Outcome and The Great Game of Business*

Tatum, Doug: *No Man's Land*

Wagner, Rodd and Harter, Jeff: 12: *The Elements of Great Managing*

Weiner, Eric: *Geography of Genius*

Wickman, Gene: *Traction*

Zook, Chris and Allen, James: *The Founder's Dilemma*

HIRE LAURIE AS A SPEAKER

Laurie Taylor has spoken to thousands of business audiences. Her topics include organizational growth, using the 7 Stages of Growth as a foundation, leadership development and employee engagement.

CRACKING THE CODE TO YOUR COMPANY'S GROWTH

Challenging insights into how companies grow based on a unique research study that shows the complexity level increases as you add people. Knowing your stage of growth provides predictability about growing a business that you can't find anywhere else.

YOUR PEOPLE ARE YOUR BUSINESS

The biggest challenge we face as business owners is the management of people. We all know people leave managers, not companies. If you address the reality that "your people are your business" early on in your company's life cycle, managing profitability, performance and productivity will be easier. Learn how to break down barriers that exist between managers and employees and create relationships that engage and encourage employees to excel.

EVERYTHING RISES AND FALLS ON LEADERSHIP

Who are the leaders in your organization? Is leadership improvement an intentional part of your company's culture? John Maxwell, the voice of leadership and author of over 70 books on the subject, identified five levels of leadership – Position, Permission, Production, People Development and Pinnacle. Learn how to apply these principles and extend your own influence as a leader to build a culture of responsibility and authenticity.

You can reach Laurie at laurie@igniteyourbiz.com.

LAURIE'S CLIENT TESTIMONIALS:

"No one knows small business in America like Laurie. There is not one of us that could not benefit from understanding and mastering the Stages of Growth concept. The Stages of Growth will identify issues you have faced, are facing and will face and can prepare you to solve current issues/address future issues and, at the same time, align your senior management team and improve communication and morale throughout your firm. I have shared with Stages of Growth with a variety of clients in a variety of industries with Laurie's help. It never fails to deliver."

-Brad Eure, Eure Consulting, LLC

"Before I tallied the evaluation forms, I knew that you were a hit! You were able to appeal to a group of business owners and top executives who are diverse in their industries, in their stage of business and in the sizes of their organizations. As I mentioned to you, this market has many one-person businesses, but I also have some of the largest employers in the region as members. You addressed the entire range with great success."

-Ken Keller, STAR Consulting

"Successful business owners will usually figure it out, but often only after it has become a problem. The Navigating the Growth Curve model is uncanny in its ability to accurately predict what is about to happen

to business owners, so they can act before it costs them time, emotional energy and money.

As for Laurie Taylor, I gave her a real challenge: give a three-hour presentation to 35 business owners and senior executives. The real challenge? Our group represented every conceivable size and type of company from startups to Fortune 50, from law firms to manufacturing to technology companies. Laurie nailed the presentation giving tremendous value to everyone in the audience. After three hours, these top executives were still in their seats and taking notes. Now that is impressive!"

-Bill McIlwaine, Renaissance Executive Forums

"Laurie's presentation received rave reviews at our annual professional conference. Several attendees commented that she was the 'best value' in the entire conference, and 'worth the price of admission!' Here are other comments we received.

- *Great presentation!*
- *Laurie was excellent. She was worth the price of the entire conference.*
- *By far the BEST presentation at this conference. Laurie's dynamic, real, humble and confident.*
- *Outstanding! I would take it again!*
- *Stars! Worth the cost of coming here alone. Extraordinary.*
- *The best value in the entire CMI conference.*
- *Very motivating and engaging, as well as a good reminder of essentials.*
- *Bring this one back next year."*

-Susan Whitcomb, Career Masters Institute

"Laurie's program is credible because she has been through growing a business as a business owner. Her presentation offered succinct tips on how to focus on my business."

-Will Temby, Greater Colorado Springs Chamber of Commerce

"Very informative and extremely eye opening! I really appreciated Laurie's honesty in talking about her own mistakes as a business owner."

-Jon Hicks, Hicks Benefit Group

"Laurie Taylor conducted a 4-hour workshop on the Stages of Growth for 30+ company CEOs, plus several of their management team. She effectively walked the entire group of companies to a clear understanding of this dynamic business model. In addition, she facilitated exercises that allowed the CEOs and their executives to begin to map out plans on how to manage their businesses. She had all parties engaged throughout the workshop.

Prior to being exposed to the Stages of Growth, some of the companies were like bumper cars bouncing around with limited forward motion, focusing on the non-important issues. The Stages are the GPS of business growth in that they provide clarity, focus and direction. Several companies that attended are now implementing the tools and processes that will lead to growth and improved profitability. I recommend Laurie Taylor and the Stages of Growth to any business entity."

-Tony Hutti, Executive Forums

ACKNOWLEDGEMENTS

It's been many years since I was in charge of a growing company. However, the memories and the experiences are so vivid it seems like yesterday. I get to share those experiences with business owners every day as I continue to work with small business owners to support their adventures of growing successful businesses.

My real joy today comes from the work I'm doing to support the over 200 business consultants and executive coaches who are now certified to share the 7 Stages of Growth concepts and my programs, The Stages of Growth X-Ray™ and Zeroing in on Your Company's Profit Zone™ with their clients.

Every month, as I work with these advisors, I hear success stories from companies that now embrace the concepts of the 7 Stages of Growth. For instance, a small, but successful manufacturing company that has been in business for over 30 years took their key employees through the X-Ray program. Now each employee is wired into helping the company make and keep more money. The X-Ray program completely changed how those employees viewed the business. The CEO is now surrounded by people who watch expenses and share in the excitement of landing new work.

Or, the CEO of a Stage 6 company who tried to sell the company twice with no results. The reason? The infrastructure wasn't in place and they had ignored some of the critical challenges in previous stages of growth. Once they had gone through the Stages of Growth X-Ray™ program, the company was sold. The new buyer retained the management team because they were doing such a great job running the company.

The reason I am passionate about writing my book series on all 7 Stages of Growth is because no other model goes into so much detail in regards to what a business owner needs to pay attention to as they grow their company. What's even more critical is the fact that this model determines your stage of growth based on how many employees you have. Understanding the impact your people have on the increased complexity of your organization completely changes how a business owner sees their company and their challenges.

I want to acknowledge all of my Growth Curve Specialists, Growth Curve Associates and my Growth Curve Strategists (a growing community of over 200 success minded business advisors) who are helping their clients to be more successful by teaching them the components that make up the 7 Stages of Growth. You know who you are and my appreciation for what you are doing to help business owners succeed grows stronger every day.

Since July 2014, my education on the world of business continues to expand because of my work as a mentor with the Southern Arizona SCORE Chapter in Tucson. It's a privilege to listen to bright and enthusiastic entrepreneurs talk about their dreams of owning their own companies. SCORE is a non-profit association dedicated to helping small businesses get off the ground and has been offering free mentoring services and educational classes for over fifty years.

I also want to again give a loud round of applause to Brooke White, my editor, whose skills and insights continue to prove invaluable in pushing me to add critical pieces of information the reader will benefit from. I appreciate her patience and her experience. Connect with her on LinkedIn, https://www.linkedin.com/in/brooke-white-3ba39a18.

My thanks also to Kim Hall, from Inhouse Design Studio, who created the front and back covers and layout for the book. Her creativity helps make these books come alive. Visit her website here: www.inhousedesignstudio.com

I'm always appreciative of James Fischer, for his research on the 7 Stages of Growth and his focus on the small business owner.

If you have ever experienced the benefits of a mastermind group, you know the value of a group of people who always have your back and who are there to help you grow and learn. I've been a part of a mastermind group for over eight years, and without their guidance and their friendship, I wouldn't be who I am today. My thanks go out to:

Tom Dearth (www.tomdearth.com)

John Marx (www.copsalive.com)

Terri Norvell (www.theinnerprize.com)

Karen Van Cleve (www.KarenVanCleve.com) and

Karyn Ruth White (www.karenruthwhite.com)

And most of all to my husband, Dave. We recently celebrated 30 years together. I love that he still makes me laugh and supports my passion for writing. (His consistent question, "How is your next book coming?" kept me focused every day.) Our love of riding motorcycles keeps us thinking young and our joy is our two Australian Shepherds, Callie and Chili, who never tire of showing us love.